EQUAL AT WORK?

WOMEN IN MEN'S JOBS

EQUAL AT WORK?

WOMEN IN MEN'S JOBS

Anna Coote

Photographs by Angela Phillips

Collins

Glasgow and London

For Clare and Emily Delap

Many thanks
to Angela Coles
for her invaluable help in finding
the subjects of this book;
to Ruth Miller
for allowing me to draw on the excellent material in
Equal Opportunities
and to Carol Marshal and Angela Coles
for their help in compiling the additional information
about jobs and training listed at the back of
the book.

First published 1979
Published by William Collins Sons and Company Limited
Copyright © text Anna Coote 1979
Copyright © photographs Angela Phillips 1979

Printed in Great Britain

ISBN   0 00 434701 3 (paperback)
ISBN   0 00 434702 1 (hardback)

Phototypeset by Tradespools Ltd, Frome, Somerset

Contents

Introduction

'Tinker tailor soldier sailor . . .' When I was a kid I used to play that game with the plum stones on my plate, hoping I'd end up with the sailor. I thought he sounded an interesting type to marry. Since I was one of three girls in the family, it didn't occur to me that boys played the game too. Only they played it differently. The number of plum stones on their plate told them what they were going to be, not whom they were going to marry.

Old myths die hard. Today there are still girls who grow up believing that the biggest events of their lives will be getting married and having children: they see employment as a kind of stop-gap between leaving school and finding true happiness with Mr Right. In fact, most girls nowadays can expect to go out to work for at least 30 years – and that allows a ten-year break for training or having children, or both.

Your job will take up as much of your time and energy as your home life, perhaps a lot more. It will also determine the *quality* of your life: being reasonably happy at home won't compensate for having to do boring, badly paid work for 20, 30 or 40 hours a week. So choosing what job to do is every bit as important as choosing whom to marry, or whether or not to have children.

When it comes to making the choice, girls seem to have a narrower set of options than boys. Unwritten rules (and some written ones) tell them that certain types of work are suitable for women while others are out of bounds. Every girl knows what the 'suitable' jobs are: nursing, teaching, hairdressing, counter sales, clerical and secretarial work, social work, catering, unskilled or semi-skilled factory work . . . Some women find these jobs really do suit them; but others just drift into them because they can't think what else to do, or they don't dare venture into a 'man's world'. They end up feeling discontented because their work doesn't offer enough challenge or reward.

There is no good reason why girls and boys should be siphoned off into separate, unequal jobs. Less than one per cent of jobs on the market today require the kind of brute force that only men can provide. Notions about men being 'naturally' more authoritative and women being 'naturally' poor at decision-taking have been thoroughly discredited.

On the other hand, there are plenty of good reasons why the barriers *should* be broken down. Women will never get equal pay while they remain segregated at work. If you need any proof of that, just look at the average hourly wages of men and women: in 1977 women were still getting 25 per cent less than men (133·9 pence an hour, compared with the male average of 177·4 pence). The Equal Pay Act states that a woman must find a man who is doing similar work to hers, for the same employer, before she can make a claim. A secretary cannot claim equal pay with the assistant office manager, even if her work is twice as valuable as his. When there are more male secretaries and more female office managers, there will be more equal pay.

If men continue to monopolize the skilled, better-paid jobs and to dominate industry, commerce, public services and government, then the traditional male values will prevail. Women will continue to be powerless to direct their own lives and the old assumptions about what they can and cannot do will live on. It would greatly improve matters if men did 'women's jobs' more often and played an equal part in looking after their homes and children. Men's horizons are often restricted by not having close contact with their children. Many of them suffer from being forced into stressful, physically exacting jobs when they'd really be better at doing what is thought of as 'women's work', such as primary school teaching or nursing.

This book is an attempt to show up the unwritten rules about what is suitable work for women. If you read on you will meet 13 young women, all very different from each other, but with two things in common: they're doing work which is normally done by men; and they love it. I've tried to select a range of jobs to suit all kinds of people and to show how each individual combines her job with the rest of her life outside working hours. In each case I have told the story of one particular woman and not attempted to give a generalized view of the job. The aim is to plant ideas in your mind and – I hope – to inspire you to consider a wider variety of ways in which you might earn your living. I am not trying to predict exactly how things will work out for you if you follow in their footsteps. If you want to be an engineer, for instance, there are a thousand and one jobs you can do and not one will be quite the same as Barbara Stephens'.

There's a reference section at the back (pp.106–128) which tells you how to apply for each job, what qualifications you need and where to train. It also lists other jobs in related fields, to help you explore further.

The women I met were pioneers and as such they were bound to be rather exceptional people. Now that frontiers have been opened up, today's generation of school leavers shouldn't need to be quite so highly motivated or highly qualified as they were (although, of course, it helps). If you want to be a car mechanic, don't give up if you haven't got a university degree like Michelle Bosc!

However, I wouldn't like to give the impression that all things are now equal between the sexes, just because 13 women have 'made it'. The majority of girls still end up doing cookery and biology at school rather than metal work or physics – and that can greatly reduce their scope when it comes to choosing a job. Employers still manage to avoid taking on women for certain types of work, often by illegal means. Women still miss out on training opportunities and get passed over for promotion. In case you find that you are being treated unfairly and not getting an equal chance to show your worth, there's a section starting on p.94 which sets out your rights under the Sex Discrimination and Equal Pay Acts.

Of course, laws are only of limited help because they cannot change people's attitudes. What we need ultimately is a society in which both men and women attach equal importance to employment, to parenthood and to domestic work, and where both have an equal chance to do what best suits their own abilities.

Barbara Stephens

Production Engineer

Barbara had not been a model pupil at Colchester Girls' High School. She disliked the hockey and the uniform and the prospect of the dull, obvious niches into which her classmates seemed destined to drop like ripe plums when they had taken their exams. Secretary nurse teacher, secretary nurse teacher . . .

She took her A-levels in English, French and history and got a place at Canterbury university to study modern history and politics, but wondered what on earth she was going to *do* with such a degree. When she sought advice none of her teachers had any suggestions that appealed to her, nor had the local Careers Office.

She might not have thought of engineering if she hadn't come across a newspaper report about a new scheme for training technician engineers. It was a four-year apprenticeship. She had all the necessary qualifications. Why not? She thought it would suit her rather well. 'I have the sort of brain that visualizes things in pictures. I'm good with my hands. I've always done well at craft – I have my own loom and still do a lot of weaving. When my sister and I were young she was good at dismantling clocks and other gadgets, and I usually managed to put them back together in the right order.' The report listed seven companies which operated the new training scheme. Barbara wrote to them all. Three failed to reply. Three said they didn't take girls*. Marconi

*This was before the 1975 Sex Discrimination Act came into force

9

invited her to their Chelmsford factory for an interview and offered her an apprenticeship on the spot.

When her friends heard the news, they all fell about laughing. 'Typical,' they said, 'trust Barbara.' Some of her teachers thought it gave the school an unfavourable image to have girls turning down university places. Her parents thought it a bit weird, but were used to surprises from Barbara and allowed her to go her own way.

At the time, she had no idea how unusual it was for a girl to train as an engineer. The report had been written by a woman and referred to 'young people', not boys. She got quite a shock when she walked in on the first day. 'It was just a sea of male faces. Two hundred adolescent boys, all staring with open-mouthed astonishment and nudging each other: "What's *she* doing here?"'

In the first year the apprentices divided their time between the technical college in Chelmsford and the training centre at Marconi. At college they studied physics, maths, the principles of electricity, elementary mechanics – all the theoretical aspects of engineering. At the training centre they were taught the basic methods of machine operation – turning, grinding, welding, sheet metal work, wiring and assembly. 'I think,' says Barbara, 'if I were more domesticated I might get the same satisfaction out of making a cake. You take a lump of metal, put it on to a machine and make it into something. You can take it home to your Mum and say "Look what I did!" When I was on sheet metal work I made a little jug from scraps of copper and brass. My Mum keeps it on her mantelpiece. When I was doing engraving and welding I made my Dad a perpetual calendar, one of those cylindrical gadgets with a knob at each end to adjust the date. He still has it on his desk at the office.'

She was living in digs in Chelmsford and going home to Colchester at weekends. It was very cold that first winter, the machine work was sometimes backbreaking and her apprentice's wage was barely enough to live on. There were consolations, however. She was fascinated by what she was learning; her parents sent food parcels; and she had bumped into Trevor Stephens, who was following a student apprenticeship* at another Chelmsford company. They started going out together and married the next summer.

'If Trevor had been a less tolerant husband it wouldn't have worked. I was too young to be married. Luckily he's a boffin type

*A sandwich course combining practical work with college study, leading to an engineering degree

who lives in a little world of his own. He doesn't care what my cooking's like as long as he's not left ravenously hungry. In fact he's got very much the same attitude as my father: "I don't care what you do as long as you're happy – because you're going to make my life hell if you're not!" Trevor was living on a student grant so we were still very hard up. But it made such a difference being able to go home to a warm bed and a warm husband and have a good moan when the day had been hard.'

In the last three years of her apprenticeship, Barbara spent half of each academic term at college and the rest of the time at Marconi, moving about from one part of the factory to another. In each department she was posted with a supervisor who taught her to do one or two specific jobs. In the Development section, for instance, where they were constructing a large rig, Barbara had to make a technical drawing of one component for the rig, then go into the workshop next door and make it up on a lathe. At the same time she was encouraged to learn as much as possible about the work that was going on around her.

The men on the shop floor were wary of her at first. Some found it hard to believe that a girl could operate a lathe. Others were certain she'd complain as soon as she got her hands dirty. It took them a few days to adjust to the idea that she was just as competent as the average boy. Gradually she ceased to be a curiosity and became simply 'the apprentice'. But before that happened there was one more hurdle to clear: the inevitable. 'Every time you go into a new workshop there's one bright spark who tries to pick you up. You can sense the danger signals – everybody pricks up their ears. Men on the shop floor have a tart and angel complex. You're either one or the other. You have to make it clear right from the beginning that you're there because you want to do the work, and you're not interested in other propositions. If you have even one or two mild flirtations, they'll all think you're easy game, and things could get very awkward for you. It's grossly unfair, but it's something I've learnt to live with.'

At college she spent more time with her fellow apprentices. There, she encountered a different kind of problem. She was two years older than most of them and it wasn't easy to make friends. 'Boys of 16 and 17 have two main interests – football and food. There comes a point where you run out of things to talk about. It might have been better if I'd been to a mixed school. An all-girls' school is no place to learn how to deal with teenage boys who don't want you around in the first place. Maybe it would have been easier if I'd known more about football, or if I'd been a dunce.'

11

Far from being a dunce, she was bright, articulate and always near the top of the class. The lecturers tended to pick her out to answer questions and the boys made their resentment clear. 'Sometimes when the atmosphere was bad I deliberately gave the wrong answer, it was easier that way.'

When she did well in the annual exams, the boys responded by sending her to Coventry for two or three days. 'In the second and third years I came top in workshop technology – that's the theory of machine work – *the* male preserve. If it had been maths it wouldn't have been so bad, but this was beating them on their own ground. It was just like going out and scoring goals on their football field!'

There were evenings when she went home vowing to give it all up. But by the following morning the prospect always seemed brighter. After all, she loved the work, especially her postings at the factory. She had plenty of support from the training officers at Marconi who were glad to have a girl on the course. 'I suppose they realized a girl wouldn't go in for engineering unless she was really keen, whereas most boys are pushed into it just as girls are pushed into shorthand and typing.'

Barbara spent the last six months of her apprenticeship in Marconi's printed circuit board plant – a small, self-contained unit where they manufacture the boards on which electronic circuits are mounted. The work is fairly specialized, involving high-precision drilling, photographic processes and silk screen printing. The plant is quieter and the work cleaner than in some other parts of the factory, and the atmosphere is friendly with everyone on first-name terms. As soon as Barbara finished ·her apprenticeship she applied for a job there as Production Engineer – and she was still there when I met her four years later.

She works in a large, brightly-lit office, one of 24 white-coated figures, some poring over circuit plans at their desks, others bustling in and out of the adjoining workshops. Approximately half of them are women employed as tracers (working from engineering drawings) and as clerks. Barbara is the only female engineer.

It is difficult to catch her in one place for more than a minute or two. She spends much of her time rushing between different parts of the plant – a tall, energetic figure with striking dark eyes and a big cheerful smile, confident, authoritative, evidently having a good time.

She's in charge of one section which comprises two clerks and another young engineer. When an order comes in she works out the most efficient and economical way of making boards to that

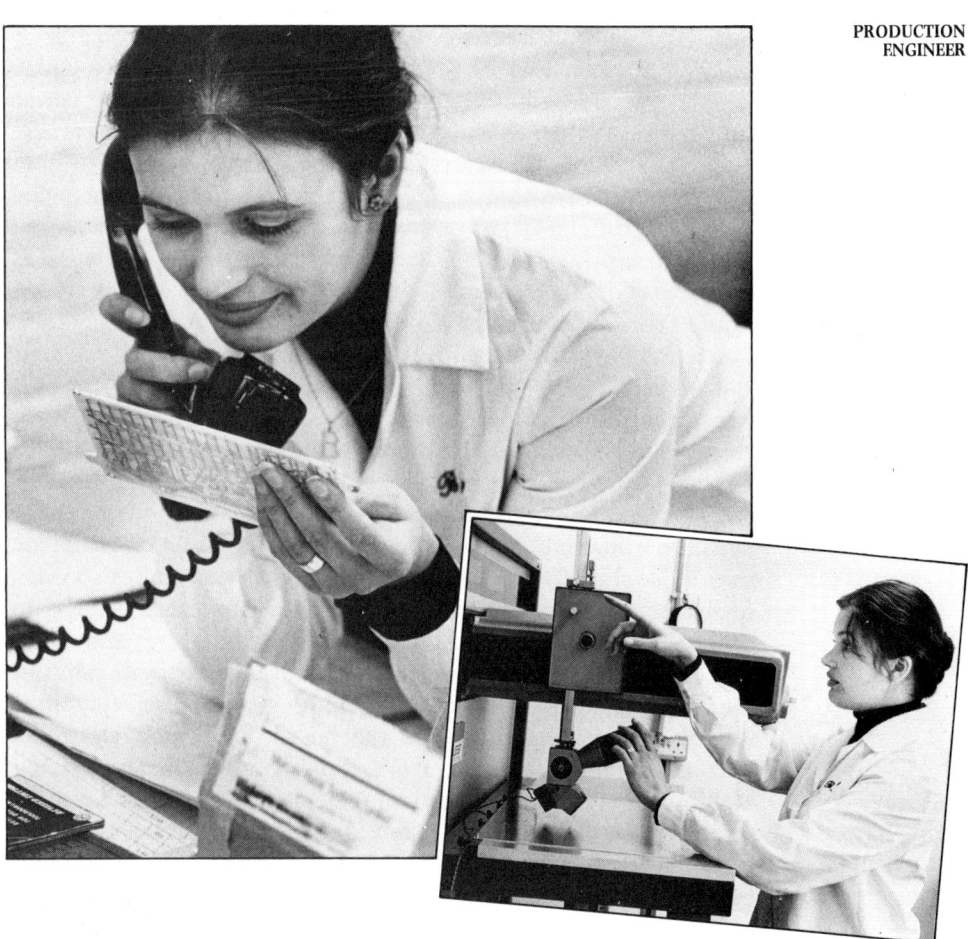

particular design. When someone on the shop floor raises a query, she either answers it herself or phones through to the customer at Coventry, Basildon or Leicester for the necessary information. She investigates new methods of production and writes reports to justify the purchase of new equipment. And when a problem crops up, she's the troubleshooter. Although she doesn't exercise the practical skills she learnt as an apprentice, they remain essential to her job: when she gives directions to shop floor workers, she has to know exactly what she is talking about. Her immediate boss, Cyril, the Production Engineering Superintendent, sits at the opposite end of the room. The unit manager, Jim, has his own glass-fronted office by the door.

An inspector from the film work section stops by her desk. 'Shop open, Barbara?' He shows her a large negative of a circuit design. 'These four holes – are we supposed to drill them?' It's an unusual design which they haven't encountered before. Barbara rings the research laboratory in Leicester, tells the technician there that the drawing isn't clear and confirms that the holes are meant to be drilled.

Jim calls her into his office. He has ordered a special consignment of material which hasn't arrived. Can she track it down? She hurries off to the store-room where she learns that the material has been checked in and dispatched to the laboratory for testing. But when she gets to the laboratory she finds that it hasn't arrived. The supervisor says he'll investigate. On her way back through the printing section, she's stopped by Pete who operates the silk screen printer. One set of boards has been badly drilled: there's 'burring' round the holes, which tears the silk screen when they're put in the printer. Barbara is not directly responsible for this department, so she consults Cyril who takes a hand drill, smoothes down the burring on one board, times the operation and decides it will be quicker and cheaper to get someone to finish the whole set by hand than to have the boards remade. Barbara then has to find someone who's free to do the work, take him up to the print room where the boards are stacked and explain what needs to be done.

Next time she passes through the drilling section she asks the drill machine operator about the fault, discovers how it occurred (the boards had been put into the machine without proper backing) and reminds the inspector in that department to let her know about any burring before passing on the boards for printing. In the workshop next door, a new piece of equipment has been installed for sharpening the drills. Barbara asks the operator how it's going. He's very pleased with it; it's easier and quicker for him to operate than the old machine. He used to sharpen up to 100 drills a day, now he can do up to 300. When it came to acquiring this equipment, Barbara had to submit a detailed 'capital expenditure request' in which she explained why it was needed, why one particular machine was preferred to others on the market, and how much it would save in time and money.

She has also carried out detailed research to find the best way of drilling circuit boards. They are made of glass reinforced with plastic and coated with copper. The holes (into which the electronic components are fixed) have to be accurate to 1000th of an inch. Barbara was trying to ascertain how fast various sizes of drill should be fed into the boards and at what speed they should rotate, in order to make the cleanest, most accurate holes in the shortest space of time.

Back in the office, a phone call comes through from the laboratory. The missing material has been traced. She reports the good news to Jim, then goes through a pile of orders on her desk. Printed circuit boards come in all different sizes: some are smaller than a pocket diary, others larger than an LP sleeve. They are built to different specifications. Some have to withstand high-speed travel, others have to be able to be dropped from a considerable height without damage. Some are expected to last for more than 50 years. Barbara decides how each new board should be made. She makes sure the work is done according to the right specifications and checks that the final product has passed inspection.

Some orders are for top secret defence projects, so Barbara knows only the code name, the design and the specifications. Others she can identify. She knows that her boards go into film cameras, television equipment, Harrier jump jets and Concorde. 'I can look at a programme on colour television, the Olympics, for instance – there were some superb live pictures coming over from Montreal – and I can say, well, one of the reasons why that picture's so good is because the boards I made are in the camera filming the event. We've just finished an order for the Moscow Olympics.' Barbara's circuit boards will be an integral part of the Digital Intercontinental Conversion Equipment (known as DICE) which will be able to convert television programmes direct from the Russian TV Standard to entirely different television systems in other parts of the world.

At five o'clock Trevor comes through to Barbara's office. He works as a Process Equipment Engineer in the same plant, looking after the computer which controls the drilling and cutting of the boards. In the evening, he and Barbara usually walk home together. Two years ago they bought a three-bedroomed house near the centre of Chelmsford. It was in a fairly dilapidated state and they're still busy renovating it, one room at a time, rewiring, plumbing, plastering, painting and decorating – doing all of it themselves. As Barbara says: 'You don't have to be an engineer to convert your own home, but it does help.'

They have a reasonable income between them now that they're both fully qualified. A lot of their money goes into the house and they've also bought a couple of motorbikes. Barbara rides a 400 cc Honda, which suits the dare-devil image she's hung on to since her schooldays.

'Luckily,' she told me, 'Trevor has no inclination to become a family man. I sometimes think it would be nice to have children but work is too exciting at the moment. I've been very happy and unexpectedly successful and I have a feeling that I shouldn't push my luck too far. If I gave up work for two or three years I'm afraid I'd lose ground. The trouble is, I don't know anybody else who's tried it yet. This is a competitive field and success depends on your practical experience.'

For the last three years she has been studying for a CNAA (Council for National Academic Awards) diploma in management studies. She goes to college every Monday to study techniques in personnel management, industrial relations, psychology and legislation affecting employment; and she's writing a thesis on the standardization of printed circuit board production.

She has a clear idea of where she's heading. Within a year or so she'll probably leave the printed circuit board plant for another department or even for another company if she's offered the right sort of work. She wants to get into line management and progress (over seven or eight years) to a unit manager's job like Jim's. She makes it sound straightforward enough. Why not?

Lesley Smith

Lorry Driver

'Have you got a single room for the night?'

'Yes, indeed, Madam.'

'Is it all right if I leave my vehicle in your car park?'

'Certainly, Madam.'

'It's the one with the 40-foot trailer behind it . . .'

It was Lesley's first long-distance trip. She had to deliver 18 tons of frozen food from a Doncaster cold store to two depots in Scotland. And it was getting late. She had made her first drop in Edinburgh and phoned through to the Glasgow depot to make sure it didn't close down for the night leaving her with a lorry full of carrots and peas. When she arrived in Glasgow it was dark. The depot was on the edge of the Gorbals and she'd heard alarming stories about the area. A small boy asked her for 10p to guard her waggon for the night and she remembered another driver telling her how he'd turned down a similar offer – and found all his wheels gone the next morning.

Most of the transport lodging houses in that part of town were full, except the ones with three beds to a room. In desperation, she headed out towards Renfrew where she was due to reload the following day, stopped at the big hotel near the airport and asked for a room for the night.

When they'd recovered their composure, the hotel staff were most helpful. Could Madam park her lorry round the back? It would be safer there. The night porter would keep an eye on it. Lesley was grateful – the vehicle was worth around £30,000.

That hotel room cost Lesley's firm £5 more than a regular stop-over, but they didn't complain as it was the first time and it never happened again. Soon she was making regular long-distance trips down to Cornwall via Avonmouth and up to Fort William in the Highlands where the roads got narrower and narrower, calling on all her skills at manoeuvring. Like the other drivers, she got to know the best lodging houses along her routes, and established her favourite transport cafés where the faces were familiar and she didn't have to keep explaining herself.

It was always the same when she went into a café for the first time. The drivers all fell silent. Then they looked out into the park for a car. When they saw no car, they assumed she was a hitch-hiker and asked her where she wanted to go. She would then explain and wait for the usual handful of jokes about women drivers. On the whole, however, the men were a lot friendlier and more courteous once they learnt that she too was a driver. They were careful with their language, and always curious. After a while Lesley wished she could carry a tape-recorded message, so she wouldn't have to answer the same questions again and again: Why did she want to be a lorry driver? How did she start? Where did she learn?

Her dad is a lorry driver, but it was never her intention to follow in his footsteps. She was brought up in a small mining village outside Doncaster, an only child and thoroughly spoilt. Her mother has worked, since well before Lesley's birth, as a nurse in the local hospital. 'My parents gave me everything I wanted. I was crazy about horses, so they saved up and bought me horses of my own. I left school at 15 without taking any exams because I was determined to start working with horses as soon as possible. I was sent to the local riding school to train as an instructor. My dad built me some stables on the land behind our house – we had a four-acre smallholding left to us by a relative. When I was 17, I started working from home, training other people's horses and giving a few free lessons to kids who helped me out in the stables.'

It was her friend Hilda who introduced her to lorry driving. An unconventional woman herself, being managing director of a local sand and gravel company, Hilda gave Lesley a rather unusual 21st birthday present: a ten-day training course for the heavy goods vehicle driving test. So Lesley went to the training centre in Rotherham and took the course to please her friend. She learnt to drive Class 1 vehicles, the biggest on the road.

The main practical skill she learnt was how to manoeuvre a large vehicle, reversing and turning a 10-ton lorry which was

12 feet wide, 40 feet long and 14 feet high – in spaces more suited to Minis and Escorts. 'When you turn a corner you don't stay close to the kerb as you do in a car. You're taught to use more of the road you're leaving than the one you're entering, and to stick to your own side of the road once you've made the turning. And you're told never to use the weight and size of your vehicle to get you around – in other words, don't play Big Brother with the little cars, they pay for use of the road too.' She had to learn the relevant sections of the Highway Code, what the law said about juggernauts, and the restrictions on hours of driving. She didn't need any detailed knowledge of motor mechanics, although she was expected to know what was wrong if, for instance, black smoke was pouring from the exhaust. In fact, she knew a lot more than that, as she had often watched her father strip down engines when she was a child.

'It's a hard test. Quite a lot of people fail. I managed to pass first go and then started to look for a job. I can't explain why – I just wanted to go on driving.'

She telephoned or visited one local company after another. 'I'll be truthful with you, love,' said one old Doncaster trucker. 'There's no way I'm going to trust twenty thousand quids' worth of my vehicle in a woman's hands.' At least he was honest. There were others who tried to fob her off by saying they might have some work in a week or two. They never did.

In the end, Lesley's father had to step in. He'd telephone a company, ask if there was a job going and find out all the details. When they said 'come and see us', he'd casually mention the job was not for him but for his daughter. Six weeks later, she was hired by a general haulage company. When the boss first saw her, he felt sure she wouldn't last for more than a fortnight. She certainly didn't look the part – a slim, delicately built young woman with pale blonde hair, dressed in neat pretty clothes. (If she turned up at your front door you might think she was the Avon lady, never the driver of a 32-ton truck.) But looks can deceive, of course, and Lesley stayed in her first job for more than a year.

Most days, she drove from Doncaster to Manchester and back, carrying nylon fabric for ICI. Occasionally she took a load of cardboard from a Huddersfield paper mill to Hull or Grimsby, where it was made into boxes. Before she could leave the yard at either end of the journey, she had to load or unload the goods. Usually there were overhead cranes or forklift trucks to help, but there were times when she had to shift cardboard by the armful and heave hundredweight bales of nylon off the back of the lorry.

When she'd loaded up, she had to throw a sheet of tarpaulin over the top and tie it tightly with rope. 'Roping and sheeting can take anything between one hour and two in good weather. If it's pouring with rain or blowing a gale it takes longer. A high wind can lift the sheet up like a balloon – I nearly got carried away with it once. The main thing is to keep the road safe, to make sure nothing falls off. You can be fined quite severely if your lorry sheds its load. I had to learn to throw a rope over a 14-foot load and to tie a special hitch called a "dolly". It took me about a week, but once you know how you never forget.

'Drivers usually help each other with roping and sheeting when they can, but most of the time you're on your own. In winter after driving all day, the knots are often thick with ice. If you manage to undo the knots, the ropes come off frozen stiff, the same shape as the load, and you have to warm them with your hands before you can bend them.' For Lesley, it was all part of the fun. A bit of discomfort in winter was nothing compared to the pleasure of being out on the road. 'Once I'd left the yard I was on my own. I'm a solitary type, so I enjoyed that. The boss couldn't contact me unless I wanted to contact him and I could work at my own speed as long as I kept to the legal limits. So if I wanted a lazy afternoon I could race around, get a day's work done in a morning and nobody was bothered.'

The driving itself wasn't physically taxing. With power steering and smooth gears, the lorry was no heavier to handle than the average family car. But power steering is a fairly recent innovation. Not long ago drivers really did need a lot of muscle, as Lesley discovered on the one occasion when she had to drive a very old vehicle. 'It was an ancient 32-ton truck. It had no power steering, there seemed to be nothing powered about it at all! I had to drive 17 miles to the Hull docks. When I came to the first roundabout I found I couldn't steer and change gear at the same time. I had to stop in the middle of the road, put it into gear, then lean on the steering wheel with all my weight to ram it round. Nowadays a child could get into a truck and steer with one hand.'

After 13 months she moved over to Hull to work for a container firm. It was easier than her last job. She picked up the loaded containers at the docks and drove them to various destinations, up to 100 miles away, where they were unloaded so she could return them empty to the docks. The only drawback was that she had to live in digs during the week. Hull was 50 miles away and she couldn't do a day's work and get back to Doncaster each night without breaking the legal limits on driving hours. (The maximum time was ten and a half hours with a half-hour break after five hours; now it's eight hours, under EEC laws.) She was very attached to her home and she missed her boyfriend Robert, a young farmer with whom she'd been going steady since she was 17. So after six months she moved back to her old firm in Doncaster.

It wasn't long before another local company offered her a better job. This was the one which took her to Scotland, delivering frozen food from the Doncaster cold store. It was the main depot for all the farmers in the area, who sent in their produce to be frozen and stored. When the produce was purchased, the farmers employed

Lesley's firm to make the deliveries which usually went in 18-ton loads to one or two customers at a time. Lesley was in charge of a larger and newer vehicle with a 40-foot refrigerated trailer which didn't need roping or sheeting.

'The only hard part was when I had to go to the North East. I don't think they'd ever heard of pallet trucks or forklifts on Tyneside. Quite often I ended up unloading 18 tons of frozen food by hand. It was packed in 24-lb boxes and I could manage two at a time. I lifted them up, carried them to the edge of the trailer and they were collected there.'

She loved the long-distance runs and was never away from home for more than two nights at a time. It was the best job she'd had so far. 'To enjoy driving you need patience more than anything. Car drivers can be very inconsiderate. They think lorries always move slowly. They'll pull out on you and make you stop and they don't realize you have to go through 13 gears before you can start again. Some car drivers even think they can get underneath a lorry! It happened to me once at a roundabout. I saw a man trying to drive underneath my trailer and I was so busy watching him that I missed the corner. I had to brake hard and pull the unit round or I'd have hit a bridge. That was the only time I ever had a slipped load. I was carrying glazed cardboard and I could feel it starting to tilt, but luckily it didn't fall.

'It's much more difficult to slow down a lorry than a car. You can't just stand on the brakes. You have to learn to control yourself in an emergency and feather the brakes [press the brake pedal up and down]. If you've got an empty trailer it's harder still. The unit may tip forward if there's no weight at the back. Most vehicles are designed to drive best with a full load – the weight slows you down as soon as you shift into neutral gear.'

By 1975, Lesley had become quite an experienced driver. That was the year in which Daf (the Dutch lorry manufacturers) and *Truck* magazine launched the first competition for women truck drivers. It was a two-day event with manoeuvring tests, a road run and written tests on the Highway Code and vehicle maintenance. There were 24 entrants but only a few of them had any working experience. Lesley walked away with first prize and soon afterwards Daf offered her a job.

She was quite happy where she was, in fact, and might not have taken the new job if she hadn't injured her knee. 'I was used to working with a 40-foot trailer and when I was unloading I knew exactly how many paces there were to the edge. One day I was put on a 20-foot trailer. I forgot and walked straight off the edge.'

A pallet truck landed on her knee and damaged the cartilage. After an operation on it, she needed lighter work while she was recovering, so she accepted the offer from Daf who employed her as a demonstrator and driver-trainer.

When customers want to buy a new truck, Lesley takes them out for a drive and shows them how to operate it. Sometimes she works from Daf's headquarters in Marlowe, and at other times she travels to the customer's company and takes their driver out for the day. Recently, she's started doing test drives, trying out new vehicles in different road conditions, recording fuel consumption, acceleration, top speeds and other factors.

It's a far cry from her previous jobs. She has a smart jacket, specially designed in the Daf colours, with a company car to match and she's working with the largest and most up-to-date vehicles on the market. She took me out in one which had a cab like a luxury caravan complete with cooker, fridge, sink, larder, wardrobe, bed and air-conditioning. It was a smooth and relatively quiet journey, and Lesley seemed to exert little physical effort in driving. But I was left in no doubt of the enormous bulk of the vehicle – by the tone of its engine and the way it dwarfed the cars on the road beside it.

Though she travels all over the country, she is still based in Doncaster with her parents and manages to get back there most nights of the week. When I last saw her she told me she and Robert were about to get engaged. 'He's been looking at houses, and we want to wait until he's found one before we get married; it may take a while because he wants to buy a small farm. Robert's been on about buying me my own lorry when we're married – just the front without the trailer – so that I could contract to pull grain vehicles and potato carts for the local farmers. There'd be plenty of work. I like the idea – as long as it would leave me time to look after Robert. I'm quite looking forward to being a housewife. Mind you, I'm like my mother. She never gave up her job, she couldn't bear to stay in the house all day.'

Roberta McDonald

Solicitor

The sun was streaming through the window. Mr Harrison leant back in his chair, clasped his hands behind his head and smiled contentedly like a man looking forward to a good meal. Across stacks of bulging files and large legal volumes covering his desk he announced cheerfully: 'Into battle we go, Miss McDonald!'

Roberta had worked late the previous night. She knew Mr Harrison was an expert in his field and the prospect of the meeting had worried her. Today she was confident. She had a long list of financial calculations in front of her and she'd read up on the relevant case law. 'Shall we start where we're in agreement – with the Specials?'

'I haven't said I *agree* with your Specials, Miss McDonald, but I may be prepared to accept them. I see your client has made some progress. How old is he?'

'He's 48.'

'Ah, so his prospects on the labour market are pretty bleak, are they?'

Roberta's client had been injured in a road accident. The driver of the car which had hit him was insured by the company for which Mr Harrison acted as solicitor. The insurance company had agreed to pay damages but not the amount. Roberta's client was a lorry driver and furniture remover. But in the accident, his leg was broken and his shoulder was permanently damaged, so that he could no longer raise his arm through more than 45 degrees. He had been out of a job ever since. Roberta had arranged this meeting with Mr Harrison to try to settle the matter out of court. Her job was to persuade the insurance company (in the person of Mr Harrison) to pay the largest possible sum of money. Mr Harrison's job was to persuade the injured lorry driver (in the person of Roberta) to accept the smallest possible sum.

The final amount would include 'Special damages' (Specials) to cover particular expenses arising from the accident, and 'General damages' (Generals), a round sum to compensate for the injury itself and future loss of earnings. The latter amount would be based upon the number of years the injured man might reasonably have been expected to earn a living, had the accident not occurred, and on his chances of getting another job now that he was disabled.

'We're primarily talking about his shoulder, aren't we?' Mr Harrison paused, thoughtfully moving his own shoulder up and down. 'It's not like losing one of the major senses – sight, hearing, touch. It's a muscular injury.'

'No, it's orthopaedic,' Roberta corrected him.

'My offer is £4000 for Generals, plus the Specials.'

'We are clearly miles apart in that case.'

'Seven years working life expectancy is the order of the day, with all the hazards a man like that has to face.'

'We're asking for eleven years. That doesn't even take him to his 60th birthday.'

'I'm not happy he can't do a job. Perhaps his old firm could employ him in another capacity. He's not legally aided is he?'

'Yes he is.' This was a trump card for Roberta. Her client's fees were being paid out of the Law Society's legal aid fund, which meant he would not be deterred from taking the matter to court by the high costs involved.

Nevertheless it was still Mr Harrison's job to reach a settlement favourable to his own client. He was enjoying himself immensely. It wasn't often he got the chance to do business with a woman. 'I'll be perfectly happy – I mean *frank* with you, Miss McDonald. My instructions are to go to £5000, but normally I like to get a bit of praise. Your client's of the artisan classes and as such he's likely to be vulnerable on the labour market. I've had a lot of experience in these matters and I ought to warn you: if you go to court the judge may well decide it's not fair to penalize insurance companies for uncertainty in the labour market.'

'Well, the fact remains that my client had a job for a very long time and he hasn't got a job now.' Roberta guessed Mr Harrison was bluffing.

'You and I have come across far worse injuries, though, haven't we? He could have an operation on his shoulder, to put in one of those plastic joints. A client of mine's got one in his hip, says it's better than the real thing.' He leaned forward. 'What's your *personal* view ?'

'My personal view is that we must be on the other side of £10,000.'

'Well, just as it's you and it's a nice afternoon, we'll stick on another £500. And there's just a possibility that I can persuade my client to overlook the £1500 we've already paid, instead of deducting it from the final sum. That's my last word. If you refuse this offer, Miss McDonald, I'm afraid I may have to ask all sorts of searching questions about your Specials . . .'

The two solicitors told each other they would seek further instructions from their respective clients. Roberta was reasonably pleased with the way the meeting had gone: Mr Harrison had improved his offer for Generals from £4000 to £7000; adding in Specials, the total came very near to £10,000. Mr Harrison was pleased. He was off on holiday. 'España,' he explained, raising his hands with an imaginary pair of castanets. 'So don't try to contact me in the next three weeks.'

Roberta works for a small firm of solicitors in Walsall, which has its front door on the high street. It is a busy practice, dealing mainly with individuals whose incomes are low enough to qualify them for legal aid. She has been there for two and a half years and is the senior of four solicitors employed by John Eccles who owns and runs the firm.

She's a tall, good-looking woman. At first meeting she seems rather cool and imposing, with her air of quiet authority and her carefully groomed appearance. In fact, she's surprisingly un-assuming – an earnest, warm-hearted soul who seems to have constructed a professional image, put it on like a hat and then forgotten all about it.

She decided to become a solicitor when she was in the sixth form at grammar school in Worthing. Lawyers and law courts had already loomed large in her life. Her parents were divorced and she, her brother and sister had been made wards of court. 'We lived in England with my father. My mother wanted us to visit her in the United States but my father refused. There was a High Court action. We children wanted to go to the States but the Judge said no, because we "might come back dissatisfied with England". He didn't ask my opinion and he referred to us all as "little children" even though I was 15!'

So Roberta had learnt at an early age that the law as it stood was not necessarily right or good, and that its effect on ordinary people's lives depended upon the skills and attitudes of lawyers. She made up her mind to become a good family solicitor.

She took a law degree at Bristol university. 'The course was about as tedious as you can imagine. It bore no resemblance to the work I am doing now. Most of the subjects were taught in a very dry way – no attempt was made to connect them with history, with social conditions or with day-to-day living. For instance, the land law course hardly mentioned the legal rights of tenants. We did have one good lecturer, in constitutional law – he didn't just tell us how the parliamentary system worked, he made us discuss its merits and its faults.' She got so fed up with the general tedium of the course that she seriously considered abandoning the law and becoming a social worker. But it proved difficult to find a job in that field, so she went on to take articles* with a firm of solicitors in Torquay, Devon. She married a friend from university – another law graduate. But while their relationship had flourished in a college climate as they studied together for their exams, it started to fall apart in the outside world. After two and a half years they separated. Roberta, now fully qualified as a solicitor, answered an advertisement in the Law Society's *Gazette* and moved to Walsall to work for John Eccles.

About 40 per cent of her clients are involved in matrimonial disputes. Of these, the majority are women. They come to her seeking separation orders, divorce, protection from assault by their husbands, custody of their children, maintenance or a share of the family property after divorce. She also handles industrial tribunal cases for people who have been unfairly dismissed from their jobs and for women who are claiming equal pay. She acts on behalf of children and young people in the juvenile courts and she appears in magistrates' and county courts to defend individuals who are being prosecuted by the police for breaking the law.

The day I visited her was fairly typical. She begins by dealing with a number of files waiting on her desk. Each file represents an individual case. The first concerns Mrs and Mr S. They have been married for 24 years with two children aged 15 and 18, and they haven't slept together for ten years. Mr S is mentally unstable and has assaulted his wife on several occasions. Mrs S wants to divorce her husband. She also wants a share of the family property which includes a substantial sum inherited from her father-in-law. Roberta

*Practical training, see p. 112

had previously spent two hours with Mrs S, taking detailed notes of all the relevant facts and circumstances which she then composed into a statement for Mrs S's approval and signature. Now she dictates a letter to Mr S explaining that his wife is taking divorce proceedings and asking (as a matter of form) about his plans for moving out of the house and paying maintenance for the children. Mrs S will see the letter before it is sent, as there is a risk that her husband may react violently. Roberta will then dispatch the letter, place a copy on file and ask the office clerk to return the file to her in two weeks' time. That way she will remember to pursue the case, even if there has been no response from the husband in the interval.

She has to record every minute of time she devotes to each case, in order to compile an accurate bill. She uses a dictating machine for all her notes and letters, as do the other solicitors. Later in the morning she interviews two applicants for a job in the audio typing pool. As senior solicitor she is responsible for hiring all clerical staff.

Another client, Mrs T, arrives late for her appointment. She is in the middle of divorce proceedings and wants to get her husband out of the house. She launches into a long story about losing her purse . . . her husband may have hidden it . . . is he trying to confuse her . . . ? Roberta listens patiently and points out that all this happened some months ago. Mrs T ploughs on relentlessly: now she has lost a letter from Roberta and her rent book . . .

her husband must have taken them . . . he'll beat her up if she accuses him . . . her daughter has been in hospital . . . is her son Gary well enough to go to scout camp at the weekend . . . ? Roberta is the only sympathetic figure of authority with whom Mrs T comes into contact. The same is true of many of her clients. Though it's her job to elicit the relevant legal factors, she is bound to play the social worker too. She reassures Mrs T. 'Don't worry about the rent book . . . ring the doctor about Gary . . . don't let your husband upset you, try to ignore him. As soon as the divorce is through we'll get him out of the house . . .' Kindly but firmly she terminates the interview.

After a quick half pint and a sandwich in a nearby pub, Roberta has an appointment at the Walsall county court, just over the road from her office. In this case, her client is a young lad who was riding an uninsured motorbike when he knocked down a pedestrian. She (the pedestrian) is suing him for damages for a badly bruised ankle and spoiled clothing. Roberta has agreed – on behalf of her client – to pay a certain sum. All that remains is to see the woman's solicitor in front of the Registrar (a senior court official) to agree to the method of payment.

The narrow corridor outside the Registrar's office is crammed almost solid with solicitors. Most of them are on matrimonial business. Spruce young men in pin-striped suits – friends and fellow club members – negotiate settlements between warring marital partners. Fragments drift from the general hubbub: 'Does she really need the single bed as well as the double bed?' 'What about the toys in the wardrobe?' 'Can't we agree to sell the house, then at least we can get him out and release £2000 for each of them?'

The queue is particularly long this afternoon. Roberta has to leave her client's file with another of her firm's solicitors who is also waiting there, and rush to Wolverhampton for her meeting with Mr Harrison. At about 6.30 she will drive home to her flat in Birmingham, then perhaps visit friends, go to the theatre or a concert or just stay in and recover from the day. Her job is fairly central to her life and she enjoys almost every aspect of it – except for the obligation to put a price on every minute of her time. If she leaves Eccles' she will probably try to join a neighbourhood law centre, where her work need not be geared to the profit motive. She is certainly pleased she didn't let the law course at Bristol discourage her. 'I'm now convinced that if you want to do something positive to help people, you can achieve more as a lawyer than as a social worker.'

Anna Cunningham

Furniture Restorer

Like Barbara Stephens, the production engineer, Anna went to a girls' grammar school where those who failed to get into university were expected to become something 'suitable' such as teacher, nurse or secretary. She passed one A-level in geography and went on to become a primary school teacher.

After six years she found her work frustrating. She seemed to spend all her time persuading other people to be creative – and that was not enough. She wanted to change direction, to achieve something more for herself. But how?

Anna would advise anyone who can't decide on a job to read the Yellow Pages. She thumbed through her local directory and picked out a list of job titles which appealed to her. She wanted to work with her hands, to learn a craft. She liked the idea of learning one of the dying crafts, such as thatching, but the idea of working with wood attracted her more. She decided to become a furniture restorer.

Having made that momentous choice, she faced the problem of getting trained. She was living in Cambridge with Bob Phillips, a student whom she later married. They had little money. Anna went round all the furniture workshops in Cambridge asking if they'd take her on as an apprentice; but they all refused. Some claimed they didn't have separate toilet facilities for women. Most of them just didn't believe she was serious. After a string of rebuffs and false starts, she lit on an adult education college which agreed to give her tuition in carpentry and let her practise in the workshop.

She could turn up when it suited her and work on her own in a corner, sawing and planing and chiselling, trying to perfect the basic techniques of the craft.

The college fees were minimal but she still had to pay her rent, so she looked for a part-time job and found one as a research assistant to an author. 'All I had to do was look up information in a library. I could do that in the evenings and on one or two days a week. The rest of the time I went to college. I had a steady income. It was ideal.'

Anna has a practical, no-nonsense style which seems to suit her chosen line of work. She is not very tall, but solidly built with strong, square carpenter's hands and an easy, unruffled manner which comes from being quite unconcerned about the way she looks or the impact she makes on other people. She's one of those women you know will always be able to cope. If she meets any difficulties, she'll discuss them dispassionately, enumerate the lessons she has learnt – and plough on, finding much to amuse and intrigue her on the way.

The first thing she was taught at college was how to cut wood straight ('true') and plane it square. She then began to construct joints: mortices, tenons and dovetail joints. She moved on to work with a wider range of woods and tools. Then her instructor told her it was time to make something.

She decided to build a sash window to replace one that was broken in her landlady's house. 'I had to make a pair of sashes because good windows should lock together perfectly. I made a plan – my first attempt at technical drawing. There are certain points of stress on a window sash where you need joints which lock more tightly as you put pressure on them; at other points of the sash you need a different type of joint. It was all very difficult. It took weeks and weeks. Finally I carried it home and fitted it. It worked! My landlady paid me £20 – not a bad bargain for a tailor-made sash window.'

Next, Anna built a filing cabinet. It was a good test of her skills, because the file drawers would not fit into the cavity without wobbling or jamming unless all their angles and dimensions were 'true'. She still has the cabinet at home and showed me how the drawers fit so perfectly that when one drawer is closed, the air inside pushes out the others.

It took her four terms at college to get that far. Then her research job came to an end. 'If you want something badly it's usually good policy to tell as many people as possible what you're looking for. I'd got to know an old boy called Ernie, who's probably

the best french polisher in Cambridge. I told him I was desperate
to find work. Ernie said he knew someone who needed help. So
I went to see Ron,'

Ron was an antique restorer with a large, chaotic business
and a barn stacked to the rafters with furniture waiting to be
repaired. He took on Anna as an unofficial apprentice – but only, he
insisted, because *Ernie* had recommended her. Ernie had said she
was serious. If it hadn't been for that, he would never have dreamt
of taking on a girl.

'He started me off stripping furniture, using a proprietary
paint stripper, then sandpaper and wire wool. After that I began to
help him with difficult jobs like glueing broken armchairs. Later
he gave me fiddly jobs like replacing veneer that had chipped off the
edges of a table. He gave me the jobs that were new to him, like
restoring ornate picture frames – I taught myself how to fill in
the damaged area with plaster, then carve it to the original shape.
Ron gave me all the jobs he didn't want to do himself. Once he
told me to repair 14 chairs which looked like they'd been in a fight
in a café.'

Ron was an exacting teacher and Anna learnt quite swiftly
to do a lot of difficult jobs. But there were some that he invariably
kept for himself. So she never learnt how to deal with a highly
polished table top, or with a badly damaged veneer.

She did learn how *not* to run a business. 'Ron was not an
enthusiastic businessman. He didn't estimate his costs properly, so
he often ended up charging too little for his work. It's vital to know
how to estimate accurately. And it's no good being frightened that
the figure you set will put off the customer. If you're not careful you
end up working at a loss – and hating it. Now I can look at a piece
of furniture and estimate, to within an hour or so, how much time
it will take me to do the job.'

After 18 months with Ron, inflation had made Anna's wage
hard to live on. He couldn't afford to give her a rise, so she had to
leave. By this time she'd learnt just enough to start up on her own.

One wild, speculative day, a friend of a friend of Anna's
bought a job lot of battered chaises longues. He asked her to repair
and re-upholster them. He also promised her more work repairing
some furniture he was buying for his own home. The chaises
longues were stored in an old factory in Haslingden, Lancashire
and, since they could not be moved to Cambridge, Anna and Bob
moved up north to settle where the work was.

Haslingden is a Pennine village that grew up in the industrial
revolution. Some of the houses are strung out along the main road

between Blackburn and Bury. The rest spill down a steep hill towards the river and the railway line. The tall brick chimneys of half a dozen cotton mills rise out of the valley. Some still operate just as they did a hundred years ago. Beyond are green hills, a few farms, then uninterrupted countryside almost all the way to Manchester.

Anna and Bob were broke, but property in Haslingden was cheap. They managed to borrow enough money to buy a small house on the main road. Its greatest asset was the basement which had a separate entrance at the back – ideal for a workshop. In the two years that followed, Anna married Bob, had a baby girl called Joanna and developed a modest but adequate business as a furniture restorer.

The work that had taken her to Haslingden ran out after a year, so she began to build up new contacts. She had cards printed: 'A. Cunningham – Antique Restorer' and delivered them to every antique dealer in the area. She put her name in the Yellow Pages. Gradually the word got round. Broken chairs, scratched and chipped tables, sunken sofas and battered chests of drawers were soon being shunted in and out of Anna's basement as fast as she could mend them.

They met with one alarming lean patch, but Bob took a job at the factory down the hill and his income kept them going while Anna decorated the house, built cupboards and fixed up some furniture for their own use. All the time she was learning more about her work. 'You must be ingenious and very patient. These are the first two requirements.' (You can tell she's been a teacher.) 'When you've learnt to handle the tools, success depends on your attitude of mind. Once I nearly ruined a valuable piece of furniture because I'd had a row with Ron and started to work in a rage.'

When I visited her she was halfway through renovating a carved rosewood piano stool. It had to be stripped and sanded to satin smoothness before being repolished. She began by rubbing it down with sandpaper, using increasingly fine grades. Then she took a wire brush to it and finally two grades of wire wool. In between each sanding she poured boiling water on the wood to bring up the grain. The stool had fine carved feet like the paws of a lioness, ending in pointed claws. One claw had been chipped off. Anna made a replica and dyed it to match the rest of the wood.

The antique dealer who'd hired Anna to repair the stool was going to make a handsome profit when he resold it. But Anna has no interest in buying and selling, and little in common with the dealers who bring her work. 'They tend to see beautiful furniture only in terms of pounds and pence. Sometimes I have to resist their inclination to over-restore things, for instance, old mahogany takes on a lovely greenish tinge and *they* tell me to get rid of it! They want everything to look new.'

She showed me a mahogany dining table she had just finished restoring. Not only had she repaired and repolished it, but she had also constructed a brand new leaf out of the side of an old mahogany wardrobe. The wood had been dyed and polished to match, and only an expert (on close inspection) would have noticed that the leaf was not part of the original table.

Anna hires a van once or twice a month to make her deliveries. 'If I'm moving a heavy piece of furniture, I check there's someone at both ends of the journey to help me. But a woman can lift as much as a man, it's just a matter of knowing how to do it.'

After two years she has a clear idea of what is needed to run a business like hers successfully. 'You've got to have a lot of confidence when you go out looking for work. You need a driving licence and you must be on the telephone. If you run a workshop from home you can get tax concessions on things like telephone and electricity costs. It's worth getting the *Which?* tax guide each year. To avoid confusion, it helps if you don't use your husband's name. People always ask for "Mister Cunningham" when they ring up, but at least I know they mean me, not Bob.'

Bob has left his factory job and is hoping to go back to college. Anna reckons she can earn just enough to support the family single-handed. When Joanna is old enough, she'll be able to play in the basement while Anna is working. 'Dust will be a problem. When I'm sanding, she'll have to wear a mask like I do. I'll make her a workbench of her own when she's about two. She should be a reasonably competent carpenter by the time she's five.'

Their house is sparsely furnished, apart from the splendid cupboards and pine-panelled bathroom which Anna installed when she ran short of work. The front room is crammed with other people's chairs and tables, so they live at the back of the house – in the kitchen where rows of nappies hang from a huge pulley over the fire and the smell of home-made bread mingles with the smell of sawdust and varnish drifting up from the cellar. Anna and Bob love having visitors – sometimes they feel a bit cut off from their friends in the south. They're both quite proud of what they've achieved so far, and besotted by their baby daughter.

In the summer when it's warm Anna takes her work out into the yard behind the house. There's a beautiful view over the valley. Joanna makes gurgling noises in the sunlight. Bob comes in with the week's shopping and starts to make lunch . . . It seems too idyllic to be true. But Anna is an exceptionally determined person. Bob was prepared to put his own ambitions aside while she established herself in business. They are both remarkably clever at making their income stretch to meet their needs. In winter it's cold and life can be a lot harder.

Fiona Fenton
Forester

The noise inside the land-rover was deafening: the back was full of big empty cans which rattled and boomed at every bump in the track. We came to a fork and Fiona stopped to consult her map.

'I've been up here once or twice before, but it's a hell of a place to get lost in. These maps aren't much use – all sorts of things aren't marked on them.' She picked the left-hand fork and drove on. If the worst came to the worst there was a radio in the land-rover. We could call her office for help. But this wave-length was also used by another group of foresters over by Inverness. She could guess what the people there would say if they overheard: 'It takes a lady forester to get lost.'

We followed the track along the edge of a field, then deep into the forest again, plunging through bracken as high as our heads. The track petered out altogether. I wondered if I could lower my voice an octave or two and call for help without prejudice. Fiona had already climbed out and was heading for a large patch of grass and scrub, bordered by rows of full-grown pine and dotted with larch trees. 'This is the spot.' She pointed to a tiny tree, not more than four inches tall, then to another a few feet away, and another. 'No wonder it was hard to find. The map doesn't show these larches.'

The young trees were planted last summer. We had come to see how they were getting on. The ground around each tree had been treated with a chemical to kill the weeds. Would the trees need spraying again? Apparently not. Most of them were still clearly visible in small, bare circles. But all was not well. The top of one small tree had been mutilated, and, instead of a single central shoot, it had put out two. It looked all set to grow into a great, forked divining rod instead of a straight, slender telegraph pole. The next tree looked much the same and the next was nothing but a poor stump.

'Deer. They love young pine trees.' There were enough deer droppings to incriminate them. They had nibbled at almost every tree, except where the bracken grew more thickly. 'Deer don't like bracken. But the bracken's a pest, too. When it dies in the winter it can crush the young trees.'

Fiona made her diagnosis: deer damage at an unacceptable level. Some of the trees might straighten out but most were beyond hope. The area would have to be 'beaten up' (replanted in patches). The deer population in that part of the forest would have to be reduced.

We drove back towards the office, thundering over the rutted tracks. It was high summer and the forest was full of wild roses, foxgloves and heather. A couple of splendid roe deer retreated up a hillside. We narrowly missed a red squirrel. All this under a deep blue sky – it was perfect, except for the flies. There were millions of flies that day. They swarmed about our heads as we walked through the trees and poured into the land-rover when we opened the door. Mercifully, they seemed to belong in the forest. By the time we had driven out of the trees and turned into the yard by the office, they'd all disappeared.

Seven foresters share the one-storey wooden office building. They are responsible for three forests (known collectively as the Laigh of Moray) which lie near the town of Elgin, halfway between Inverness and Aberdeen on the north-east coast of Scotland. Across the road from the offices, down a short track, is a row of cottages. The end one is Fiona's. Three bedrooms, a living room, kitchen, bathroom and garden. She lives there all on her own except for her Irish terrier, Teddy. The house comes with the job.

Not that she'd have chosen to live that way. She is 23 and married. Her husband, Glen, works near London. Her parents live in Ulster. But it wasn't easy to get the sort of job she wanted. It took her a year to find this one, after she'd got her degree. She was the first woman forester to be employed by the Forestry Commission – and when I met her she was still the only one.

The seven foresters at the Laigh of Moray are divided into three sections, each with different responsibilities. There is one head forester and one ordinary forester (Fiona's rank) in each section, with one chief forester over all.

The Plant Production section runs the nursery, taking seeds from orchard trees grown for the purpose, sewing and nurturing them until they are ready to be planted out in the forest. The Harvesting and Marketing section arranges for the trees to be felled, taken out of the forest and sold. The Forest Management section, where Fiona works, looks after the trees from the time they are planted to the time they are ready to be felled. This involves preparing the ground before planting, planting out the seedlings, weeding, draining, fencing, fertilizing, organizing fire protection, looking after wildlife and laying on facilities for the public, such as picnic areas. (In the course of her training with the Forestry Commission, Fiona will spend some time in all three sections.)

In each section the foresters work with a squad of labourers. Earlier that day we had driven out to another part of the forest to meet her Management squad. Fiona had delivered some paraquat, a very powerful weed-killer, for spraying on the ground round some young spruce trees. She brought the squad knapsack sprayers and protective clothing including wellington boots and eye shields. She gave them a measuring jug and told them how much water to add to the concentrate. Finally she handed them each a sheet of paper on which she had written all the safety precautions they were supposed to take. Here were three tough old Scotsmen who'd lived and worked in the forest for most of their lives, taking instructions from a 'wee lassie' just out of college. It was all very amicable. They were used to Fiona by now.

'Technically I'm their boss but of course that doesn't mean I boss them around. They know far more about the area than I do — and about their particular job. I move them from one operation to another, work out what equipment they need and explain what they have to do in non-technical terms. They tell me if they foresee any difficulties and we work out a solution together. Obviously, their advice is invaluable and they always have a say in how a job is executed.' Later that afternoon a message came through to Fiona at the office. The squad couldn't locate the spruce trees — they were already too overgrown with weeds. She would need to go back and inspect the plantation. The men would probably have to start weeding by hand and spray afterwards. If the paraquat were to touch the young spruce it would kill them. The men knew this already, and Fiona would simply give the go-ahead, make sure they had the right equipment, then check that the work was proceeding without any problems.

Fiona took a course in forestry at Bangor university on the north-west coast of Wales and got a second-class honours degree.

Her interest was first encouraged by her father, a botanist who used to lecture at Queen's University, Belfast. Her mother runs a chicken farm, and the family have always lived in the country. Fiona was sent to two girls' boarding schools, first in the Irish Republic, then in Belfast.

She is a quiet, independent sort of person – one who will probably always surprise friends and family by being less conventional and more successful than they had expected. 'I wanted a job out of doors, a practical job. I thought about agriculture but that can be difficult: either you own a farm or you're just a farm worker and there's not much future in that. I suppose I chose forestry because I hoped I'd get a job just like this one.'

Her course at Bangor involved the study of forestry throughout the world, as many of the students intended to work overseas, especially in Africa. She learnt about the zoology and botany of forests; how to plan and survey a new forest and to build (in theory, at least) roads, drains and bridges. She studied the structure of wood and the operation of the timber industry; the economics of forestry and techniques for nurturing and harvesting trees. The students were sent on field trips to study private and Government-owned forests in Britain, and on a visit to Europe (Fiona went to Norway) to observe forestry techniques abroad.

She met her husband at university. Now he's a biology teacher and has a good job at a school in Essex. They both agreed it would be best if he didn't leave his job to join Fiona in Elgin, and he comes to see her about once every four weeks.

'My social life is not exactly hectic here. The pubs in Scotland are still very much a man's world. If I were a bloke I'd be able to walk in and say "how about a game of darts" – I'd certainly have made more friends. I go horse riding in the summer and there are a few people I visit. In fact, I'm kept busy enough looking after the house and the garden, growing vegetables and going for walks with Teddy.'

She gets on well with her colleagues and loves her work. She has plenty of opportunity to study wildlife, which is her main passion. Sometimes she gets up before dawn and goes out with the forest ranger, Bill, when he's counting the deer. Bill is responsible for all the animals in the forest. His job involves looking out for poachers, controlling vermin, protecting some of the less common species and keeping the deer population at a steady level. 'The deer are shot at certain times of year. Now it's the bucks; in winter we cull the doe. We have to remove about 160 head a year to keep the stock steady and we choose the poorest specimens for the cull. Stalkers come and pay us for a licence to shoot the deer. Bill goes out and supervises them. When they shoot a deer they can take the head home as a trophy. They have to pay for it, though, according to the antler size. We keep the carcasses and sell them to a licensed game dealer in Inverness.' It's part of Fiona's job to organize the hunters and assess the antlers for payment.

Once a week she takes a public coach tour round Culbin forest which is quite a curiosity. 'It used to be a rich agricultural estate until the 17th century when sand began to encroach on the farmland. This was partly due to a series of storms and partly due to the fact that people had been pulling up marram grass from the sandhills to make thatch. Within a generation the whole estate was buried under sand, including the manor-house and 16 crofts. The Forestry Commission acquired the land in the 1920s and set about planting it. They had to cut down brushwood, pin it to the sand like thatch and plant trees in between. A lot of people who used to live nearby come back to see it. They can't believe their eyes – they remember Culbin as a huge desert of shifting sand. A camel wouldn't have looked out of place there.'

One thing Fiona does not enjoy is filling in time sheets for the Management squad. Every task is listed and allotted a code which is fed into the computer at the Commission's headquarters in Edinburgh, so that wages can be charged to a particular account number. She has to mark down what each member of the squad does each day and for how many hours – clearing scrub, weeding, fencing, spraying, and so on. Accounting and other office work take up a lot of her time.

In many ways Fiona's is an administrative job. That's something she didn't learn much about at college. The Commission sent her on a training course where she learnt about general management principles, incentive schemes, delegation of work, budgeting, and how to plan and cost different jobs. They sent her on a chain sawing course too, and kitted her out with a pair of regulation boots, specially reinforced at the front. But unfortunately the boots weren't made with women in mind, so she has to clump around in size 7s.

As a general rule foresters who work for the Commission are expected to move from one forest to another about once every five years. This enables them to broaden their experience and it's often necessary for promotion. But it has caused problems for some foresters whose wives have established themselves in jobs and whose children may have reached a very important stage in their schooling.

Some foresters have been trying to change this rule by negotiating through their union and the arrival of a forester with a *husband* cast a different light on the issue. When Fiona asked to be transferred to Thetford, a forest in East Anglia, where she would at least be able to see Glen every weekend, the union backed her and the Commission eventually agreed. Her case may set a useful precedent for male foresters in future.

So three months after I met her, Fiona moved south. She is now in charge of a nursery, growing Corsican pine seedlings in a controlled environment until they are ready to be planted out in the forest. Her aim is to become a wildlife forester. That would involve building up a specialist knowledge of wildlife and conservation and acting as a consultant for a group of forests. With any luck, Glen will get a job near Thetford one day and they'll be able to live together.

Claudine Eccleston

Plumber

The pick-up truck was waiting at the depot door. Claudine came out carrying the washbasin, lifted it over the side of the truck and climbed in after it. 'Ah, look what power she has! What a woman!' exclaimed her workmate Charlie (who stood no higher than her nose) with mock reverence and some genuine admiration. I heaved myself into the truck beside her, less nimbly, carrying her tool-bag.

'Why don't you ladies come with me?' Charlie demanded. 'I'll give you a lift in my car.' He sidled up to where Claudine sat, put his chin over the edge of the truck and closed his eyes. 'Give us a kiss?'

'He's not usually like this – he must be showing off,' Claudine told me, giving him a friendly push as the truck began to move. 'Hold on tight – you'll need to.'

It was just after nine o'clock on a December morning. We rode off up the hill through thick, icy fog and stopped outside a tall block of flats. 'They'd better be in,' said Claudine after the truck had disappeared back into the fog. She led the way up the steps to the main entrance, bearing the basin and looking rather stately in her full, funky-coloured coat and black beret. 'You know,' she said, with one of her lop-sided smiles, 'they call me the best-dressed plumber in the borough.'

We took the lift to the 20th floor. A small boy in pyjamas opened the door. 'Mum! It's the plumber.' Claudine had visited this flat before, but sometimes she had difficulty persuading council

43

tenants that she really was the plumber. One elderly couple were so incredulous that she had to go back to the depot for a note of authorization before they'd let her over the threshold.

The boy's mother, Mrs O'Brien, had first complained to the council about the washbasin 18 months ago. In fact, she told us, it had been cracked when she moved in five years ago. For the last six months it had been too leaky to use at all, which was no joke when you had five children, two of them little ones. She was glad to see Claudine who, she knew, was not to blame for the delay. 'Go into the kitchen, dear. Liam!' (to the boy) 'put the kettle on and make the girls a cup of tea while I take this washing out of the bath.'

In the tiny, narrow kitchen, Liam's five-year-old sister abandoned her toast at this new, unexpected source of interest and began to pummel us with questions. 'Have you had *your* breakfast? What's your name? Are you working? What's this? Is it yours?' Claudine answered each question patiently as she took off her coat and clambered into a voluminous pair of dungarees. 'They let you keep these when you've finished at the Skill Centre. There were only two sizes, large and medium. I got the big size, don't ask me why.'

Claudine trained to be a plumber by taking a six-month TOPS* course at one of the Government Skill Centres. Two years ago, at 21, she decided it was time she learnt a proper trade. She could type but had tried a couple of office jobs and hated them. They were badly paid and she was bored stiff sitting indoors all day, doing other people's work.

She might have done better at school if she hadn't been the eldest of seven children and proxy mother to them all. She was in the 'A' stream of her south-London comprehensive school, but when she should have been studying for exams she had to do the shopping and cleaning, cook supper for the whole family and wash the dishes before she could start her homework. Her mother was a bus conductress, her dad a carpenter, but even when they were both in work they couldn't earn enough to keep a family of nine. So her mother also put in a four-hour evening shift at a toy factory and Claudine failed all her O-levels, despite the promise she had shown.

When she was 16 she had a blazing row with her mother and was turned out of home with her belongings in a laundry bag and nowhere to go. After some adventures she prefers not to

*See pp. 92–3 for further information on TOPS

publish, the local authority sent her to live with foster parents. Only then did she go to college and pass three O-levels. She stayed on to study for A-levels, but gave up before the exams, still frightened of failure.

She left her foster parents and lived with friends from college, squatting in empty houses in different parts of town. She'd always liked working with children and now she took a series of temporary jobs with holiday play schemes. She found she enjoyed working with her hands, doing crafts and painting with the kids. A lot of the men she knew were in manual jobs; some were printers and some were on building sites, working as bricklayers, joiners and plumbers. They told her the pay was good. The work they were doing appealed to her and so she decided to learn a manual skill. She was too old to start an apprenticeship and she didn't want to spend four years at night school. The quickest and cheapest way to train was to take a Government-sponsored course.

'I went down to the Labour Exchange and looked through all their little leaflets. There were three courses I was interested in – printing, carpentry and plumbing. I knew a lot of guys who were printers, so I decided if I really wanted to print I could learn from them in my spare time. What swayed me towards plumbing was that in all the places I'd lived, I'd never had to call in a carpenter. There's always somebody around who can do a bit of woodwork. I liked the idea of not having to call in a plumber, even in an emergency. And I didn't think I could learn it from my friends.' She filled in the application form and prepared for a long wait.

In the meantime, she took a job on a building site. It wasn't hard to get work. She and her friend, Patti, turned up at the site one morning and offered their services. The supervisor tried to avoid them at first, but eventually took them on as painters and decorators. He'd heard about the Sex Discrimination Act and didn't want any trouble.

Claudine liked the work and the pay was better than in any of her previous jobs, but she wasn't allowed to forget that she had intruded on a man's world. There was the architect who came in drunk after a long lunch and 'flashed' at Claudine. And there was the foreman who kept making passes at her and turned unpleasant when she rejected them. One day she had a bitter argument with him while they were up on some scaffolding painting the front of a building. She swore at him. He reported her and she was fired. As Claudine says: 'No man would have been fired for swearing at a foreman on a building site – at a supervisor or site manager, perhaps, but not at a foreman.'

Luckily, it wasn't much of a setback. She spent the summer picking grapes in France and the following October was called for an interview at the Skill Centre. They gave her a place on a course beginning the next April. The experience she'd gained of construction work turned out to be an asset. It was a big help during the interview when she was asked to write a short essay about conditions on a building site; and it gave her more confidence in dealing with her fellow students.

Claudine was surprised to discover that plumbing was such a complicated business. It wasn't just a matter of joining pipes or mending leaks. She was also taught how to plan and fit central heating, to fit gas cookers and heaters, to install baths, sinks, lavatories and boilers, to construct guttering, to weatherproof roofs and to lay drains. And she learnt to do each job in the full range of materials: lead, copper, zinc, aluminium and PVC.

The quality of the teaching impressed her and she only wished the course could have gone on longer, to let the students finish as fully qualified plumbers. As it was, she emerged after six months with skills at a standard she might have attained after two years at night school. It was enough to get her a job as a trainee plumber – though not without difficulty.

'I heard Camden Council was looking for plumbers. I'd already decided I wanted to work for a public body and the Council was my first choice. I went to see the personnel officer three times and each time she told me there were no vacancies. I told the union convener what had happened. He went up and asked if she had any jobs for plumbers. She said "yes" – and after that she had to hire me.'

Claudine is based at the building office in Primrose Hill Court, along with all the plumbers, carpenters, builders and decorators who work in that area of the borough. It's a bustling warren of a place; the corridors are stacked with pieces of timber and cans of paint and kitchen units en route for various council properties. There's a cheerful, easy-going atmosphere and a warm smell of freshly sawn wood. The men aren't in the least put out by Claudine's presence. They like her: she's one of their mates. 'It's amazing how quickly attitudes have changed,' she told me, 'even in the last 18 months. It's no longer an unheard of thing for a woman to be doing this sort of work. Some of the men are even beginning to get *used* to the idea!'

Although she's still a trainee, she does the same work as the other plumbers – fitting sinks, baths and lavatories; unblocking drains; mending leaks and broken washers, cisterns and tanks.

She would like to go to college one day a week to study for the City and Guilds exam, but the Council will only release her on condition that she loses a day's pay. She thinks this most unfair – and too high a price to pay for a paper qualification. In 14 months she will get a full wage as a maintenance plumber and that's good enough for her.

There's a bonus system of payment based on the amount of work done within certain time limits. Each job is allotted a number of hours. 'It's ridiculous,' Claudine remarked when she had unscrewed the cracked basin from the wall of Mrs O'Brien's bathroom. 'They allow us six hours to fit a kitchen sink and only two hours for a washbasin, which needs just as much work. I'll be lucky if I get this done in a day.'

Since bathroom fittings are not built to any standard design, the holes for the taps in Mrs O'Brien's new washbasin did not meet the pipes coming out of the wall, and the wastepipe was too long

to meet the plughole because the new basin was deeper than the old. Claudine perched on the edge of the bath and considered the problem. How much new pipe would she need? And how many 'elbows' (L-shaped joints)? Should she fit a new S-bend or cut a bit off the old one? 'I never thought plumbing would tax my brain like this. I'm sure I use it more now than I ever did at college.'

We left the basin and the tool-bag, gave solemn promise to return within an hour, and walked back down the hill to the depot. We collected some extra equipment, told the foreman the job would take more than two hours, had a quick cup of tea and plodded up the hill again. Then Claudine got down to the intricate business of measuring the pipes, cutting them to size, working out the angles of the joints and soldering them together. Each length of pipe had to be right to within a couple of millimetres. Each joint had to be solid and watertight, not just today but in 20 and 40 years' time.

The little O'Briens were still frisking around, full of curiosity. (It was a school holiday.) 'How did you do that?' the girl demanded as Claudine turned on her gas torch. 'Magic,' she replied solemnly. 'There's a lot of magic in this game. What did you say your name was?' 'Ruth.' 'You will not be my friend much longer, Ruth, if you don't go away. Why don't you watch television?' Claudine went on sawing and soldering and struggling with the pipes underneath the basin. Slow, careful, endlessly patient. She'd have done the job more quickly if she'd had some proper metal cutters instead of just a hacksaw. But plumbers have to buy their own tools and she hadn't saved up enough for them yet.

By mid-afternoon the basin was installed. 'Now for the big moment, folks.' Claudine turned on the water supply and tested the taps gingerly. The water flowed dutifully from the taps and disappeared down the drain. Magic. We carried the remains of the old basin downstairs and left it by the road for the truck to collect later. It was too late for Claudine to start another job that day, so we left her tools at the depot, bought a cherry cake and caught the bus back to her place for tea.

Her evenings are often busier than her days. She's the singer in a rock band. Of course, there's always the possibility, she says with an ironic grin, that she may be forced to give up plumbing when she gets to be a star. Whatever she does in the future, it's unlikely to be conventional. She has no intention of marrying her current boyfriend or anyone else. She shares a big house in Tufnell Park with four friends. It's her first permanent home since she left her parents. And they never have to call in a plumber.

Marilyn Booth

Airline Pilot

'Have you seen the herb market in Teheran? There's one little man who sells nothing but chives and another who sells only rosemary . . .' Captain Joe Wright sat on the left-hand pillow, leaned against the bedhead, stretched his legs out (shoes carefully off the coverlet) and drank his beer from the toothmug. He looked for all the world like an airline pilot in a Hollywood movie.

Three stewardesses sat on the other three corners of the bed, a fourth in the easy chair. They all looked tired and a bit rumpled. On the floor by the door a young trainee engineer stared silently into his drink, too shy or too exhausted to join in the conversation. On the stool at the end of the bed perched the flight engineer, an exuberant gnome-like creature with a big bushy beard. Beside him sat Marilyn Booth, First Officer, a slim young woman who sipped her Scotch contentedly and said little.

Their shift had begun at Gatwick Airport, shortly after eight that morning. Now it was six o'clock in the evening and they'd just arrived at the Excelsior, Birmingham Airport's main hotel – by way of Milan, North Italy and the East Midlands Airport near Derby. They were setting about their first drink with some relish, unwinding gradually, enjoying the Captain's Middle Eastern tales and looking forward to as good a time as could be had on a Saturday evening in Brum. They would not be working again until the Munich flight took off on Sunday afternoon.

Marilyn told me that if she ever stopped being a pilot she'd like to work in television. As a producer or a camerawoman,

49

perhaps. She'd once spent three days making a film with a television crew and she'd been struck by the similarity between their teamwork and sense of camaraderie and those of an airline crew. They lived and worked together in an all-absorbing way – even though they might not see each other for weeks or months afterwards. It was something she particularly liked about her present job.

Marilyn first caught the travel bug when she was 13. Her parents, who owned a clothing shop in Bradford, took her on a sea cruise to Casablanca. It was her first trip abroad and she was enchanted. She left school at 16 with a handful of O-levels and wrote to all the airlines asking for a job as a stewardess. They told her she couldn't work on aeroplanes until she was 21, so she spent the intervening years learning German as an au pair in Austria, and Spanish as a hotel receptionist in a small town near Barcelona. As soon as she was old enough she joined Britannia Airways and worked as a stewardess on flights out of Luton airport to Mediterranean resorts and most of the major European cities.

It wasn't long before the aeroplanes themselves began to fascinate her more than their destinations. She had a boyfriend who was a pilot with Britannia and she went out on training flights with him while he was teaching other pilots to fly new aircraft. 'We'd just got the 737s. They were lovely aeroplanes, very new, very powerful and we were doing simulated one-engine take-offs in them. It was so *exciting*. I was determined to learn to fly after that.'

Unfortunately, training for a pilot's licence is prohibitively expensive and Marilyn had to take steps to raise the necessary funds. She left Britannia Airways and travelled round Australia and New Zealand with a girl friend. They worked as barmaids, waitresses and cleaners while Marilyn saved up enough money to train for her private pilot's licence in New Zealand, where the course was relatively cheap. She flew every day for six weeks in a small single-engine plane and passed her test the day before the boat left for England.

Back home again, she went to work for Dan Air as a senior stewardess and it was soon clear to all her colleagues that she wasn't going to be satisfied with flying small private aircraft. She wanted to get her hands on the big passenger planes. Whenever she had a moment free from serving meals, pouring drinks and selling duty-free cigarettes, she'd be on the flight deck, watching avidly, asking questions. She learnt from the Chief Stewardess that Dan Air sponsored two people each year to train for their commercial pilot's licence. She applied. The first year she was turned down. From then on, she says, she made an absolute nuisance of herself lobbying the Chief Pilot mercilessly, spending even more time on the flight deck while she was working and, while she was not, spending every available moment on Dan Air's flight simulator which the company uses to train and test pilots. It worked. Dan Air advanced her £1000 towards the cost of the course (she'd borrowed the rest from friends*) and promised her a job when she qualified.

She spent a year at the Oxford Air Training College – the only woman among 200 men. She needn't have worried about her total lack of scientific or mechanical knowledge – it turned out that most of the men knew as little as she did. And while her private pilot's licence probably helped her get the Dan Air sponsorship, it wasn't a prerequisite of the course. One of the students confessed that he had never been in an aeroplane in his life, not even as a passenger!

Weather permitting, she spent every other day flying Cherokees – small, four-seater single-engine planes. The rest of the time she learnt about the structure of aircraft, their engines, their electrical and radio systems, and about meteorology, radar and navigation. At the end of the course she took a set of written exams and a series of practical flying tests with an examiner from the Department of the Environment. When she'd passed all these, she got her commercial pilot's licence, but in order to work for Dan Air (and for most other airlines) she needed a further 35 hours' practical training to get her 'Instrument Rating' which meant reaching a certain level of competence in handling all the instruments in the aeroplane.

She began her career as a pilot on Dan Air's fleet of Hawker Siddeley 748s. These are the company's smallest passenger planes, used mainly on internal flights hopping between Aberdeen, Glasgow, Newcastle, Liverpool and Bristol. After two years she transferred to the Comet fleet. Most pilots work on only one type of aircraft at a time. Before transferring to a new plane, they have to go through several weeks' training in ground school, on the flight simulator and in the aircraft itself. They need a special stamp on their licence to prove they can fly each type of aeroplane.

When I met Marilyn she had been with the Comet fleet for two and a half years. She does about 650 hours' flying a year, which is the limit set by her union. Since Dan Air's main business is holiday charters and the company uses Comets on all its busiest routes, she does most of her flying in the six months between April and October, and the rest at weekends and winter holiday times.

*See p. 120 for the cost of learning to fly commercial aircraft

I flew with her to Milan when she was taking skiers to and from the Italian Alps. In the summer she flies to Mediterranean resorts, occasionally to North Africa, and in the last two years she has had only two stop-overs outside the UK. My vision of off-duty pilots lounging on exotic beaches was a long way off the mark. But then Marilyn was never attracted to her job by any hope of a glamorous life. She was captured (and still is) by the sheer excitement of causing a large, powerful aeroplane to get off the ground and fly.

Dan Air insists that all pilots who are based at Gatwick should live within two hours' travel of the airport, so they can be summoned at short notice. Marilyn owns a small house in Reigate, about an hour's drive away. She lives on her own and prefers it to sharing with friends. 'I come in from work at all sorts of odd hours and I'm usually exhausted. The last thing I want when I get home is to find someone else having a spring clean, or an unexpected guest staying in my room.'

The day of our Milan flight was fairly typical. She left home at 7.30 in the morning. As soon as she got to Gatwick she called in at the Dan Air operations room for the flight plan, and then to the Met. office for details about the weather. 'I look at the winds and work out how much fuel we're going to need. I have to estimate whether it's cheaper to take enough for the return journey or to refuel when we get there. The Captain checks my calculations, then I ring up the engineer who phones the fuel order through to Shell.' We took $14\frac{1}{2}$ tons of fuel with us to Milan – enough to get us there and back.

Next, she checked out the route for potential hazards. 'It's all a bit like motorways. Everyone flies along set routes. There are beacons on the ground which radiate signals and we hop from one to another. Sometimes there's a beacon out of service and we have to work from the next one instead. We have to find out if there is likely to be any turbulence and whether there's snow or ice on the runway. Sometimes military exercises are in operation over the whole of France and we have to use a lot of extra fuel flying round them.'

A large part of Marilyn's job consists of rigorous, methodical attention to detail. She has the sort of rock-steady temperament and low-key approach which suits her work ideally. As First Officer, she is responsible for most of the pre-flight checks on the aeroplane.

'I check all the warning horns, the controls and the radios. The engineer has his own checklist. We both reach a certain point on our lists and by that time the Captain is in his seat and the three of us do the rest of the checks together. The senior hostess tells us when she's got all the passengers on board, then I call up airport control and ask for clearance to start.'

As they begin to taxi on to the runway, the engineer reads out another list of checks which can be made only when the engines are running. With their eyes glued to the instrument panels and the runway ahead of them, the two pilots go through an Incapacitation Drill in which certain calls are made and acknowledged aloud ('Airspeed building' . . . 'Confirmed', and so on). The idea is that if one of them became incapacitated and failed to reply, the other would notice immediately. Marilyn explained that although this was very unlikely to happen, it was just possible that one pilot could go into a coma or have a heart attack without showing any outward sign. If they didn't have the drill, the other pilot might not notice until it was too late.

As they're taking off they are only allowed to say certain essential things because everyone is listening for one word: 'stop' – the signal that something is wrong. If they hear it, they all have to

react extremely fast, because once the aeroplane has reached a certain speed, they can no longer bring it to a halt before the end of the runway. This has happened only once in Marilyn's career, when an engine failed to build up sufficient power for take-off. As the signal came the aeroplane was moving relatively slowly, 40 mph, so the crew had no difficulty in stopping in good time.

'Once we are airborne and begin to climb, the idea is that we do as little as possible, just concentrate on flying. I have to operate a thing called a "roll damper" which prevents the aeroplane from rolling too much, switch off a pump and the No Smoking signs, and press a button which brings up the wheels. When we're coming out of Gatwick we're restricted by Mandatory Noise Abatement, which means we have to reduce our engine power to cut down the noise. We also have to change frequencies on the radio so that we're talking to the main control centre near Heathrow Airport which controls air traffic from Scotland all the way to France by means of radar.'

The contrast between the passenger deck and the flight deck on the Comet was startling. I left the rows of holidaymakers on upholstered seats and passed through two orange curtains and the narrow galley from which the stewardesses would soon conjure more than 100 hot meals. Suddenly I was in a tiny cluttered bolt-hole of a cockpit. There were banks of dials and knobs which might have been collected from the dashboards of a hundred vintage racing cars. The roof was swathed in khaki-coloured quilted fabric which dripped with condensation. Marilyn and Joe were at twin control panels set into the tip of the Comet's nose. The trainee engineer was sitting behind Marilyn, reading another huge panel of instruments and tapping out figures on his pocket calculator. There was just enough room for the flight engineer to squeeze in behind the Captain.

When the plane had reached cruising height and they'd switched to automatic pilot, there wasn't much work for Marilyn and Joe to do. They noted down reports from each of the weather stations they passed, in case they had to make an unscheduled landing. They drank cups of tea – one every 20 minutes (the atmosphere in a plane is so much drier than at sea level that flight crews who are constantly exposed to it need to replace liquid regularly to guard against kidney trouble). They glanced out of the window from time to time and when the Alps began to perforate the clouds, the Captain reminded the passengers over the intercom to look out for Mont Blanc. The crew ate their dinner – a different type of food, separately cooked for each member as a precaution against food poisoning. It was odd to watch the pilot of a large plane carrying 119 passengers across France and Switzerland at a height of $4\frac{1}{2}$ miles, sitting sideways in her chair, tucking into a dish of chicken curry and occasionally reaching out to twiddle a knob which made the sky tilt this way or that. I'd imagined she would spend every minute of the flight hunched eagerly over the steering gear, nose to the windscreen, teeth gritted with determination (and probably even going 'vroom vroom'). Only when she switched off the automatic pilot for the descent to Milan did it start to look as if there were some direct relationship between the passage through the air of that great metal bird and the two people sitting up at the front.

When the Comet had come to a standstill and the stewardesses had bid farewell to the skiers, the two pilots took a short walk across the tarmac to the Met. office for the latest weather report, then returned to the plane. We were due to take off again in an hour. But the coaches were late bringing in the next consignment of passengers and we were delayed for 90 minutes. The crew settled down in the front seats of the passenger deck. Joe gave Marilyn a lesson in knotting her tie. One of the stewardesses was celebrating her birthday. The time passed quickly and we were all engrossed in conversation when a crocodile of small boys clutching boarding cards began to file in through the rear door. The crew leapt into action. Two hours later, Marilyn brought the plane down at Derby and a fleet of taxis ferried us twenty-odd miles to the Excelsior hotel at Birmingham Airport.

When she gets home from a flight, Marilyn's friends often ask her what it was like in Milan or Madrid or wherever she has been that day. Usually she can't tell them, she scarcely noticed. She has done so much travelling in the 18 years since her cruise to Casablanca that although she still enjoys the process of travelling, the sights of foreign countries no longer catch her interest. When she went to Khartoum for a holiday last autumn it was only because she'd been there before, liked the hotel and wanted a good rest in the sun after an exhausting summer. Apart from her six weeks' holiday each year, flying totally dominates her life. 'Last year I decided I would make a determined effort to get out and meet people. It's been a complete failure,' she said without much sign of regret. 'I joined a squash club, but keep having to cancel my games. Sometimes I don't even have a chance to ring up and apologize. If I've arranged to visit a friend and Dan Air ask me to fly, I'll fly. Because I like it. People find that very hard to understand.'

It will soon be time for her to move on from the Comet fleet although they're her favourite planes and she'll be sorry to leave them. Last year she got her senior pilot's licence which means she can now be promoted to Captain. But the airline's pecking order is very precise. As a junior Captain, she will have to start on the 748s and will probably be based in Aberdeen for at least a year until someone more junior relieves her.

Every six months she takes a test on the flight simulator and every year she has a medical examination. If she fails, she will lose her licence; if she passes she can go on flying until she is 55 or 60. 'At the moment I'm not sure I want to. I feel like a change. I always said I'd never do a job that ties me down. I couldn't have chosen a less likely profession, could I?'

Liane Bracken

Sales Representative

At 8.30 in the morning, Liane emerges from her pretty, modern house in the village of Dore outside Sheffield. She is smartly dressed and carries a shining black briefcase. Her husband Barry has already taken the bus into the city where he works for an insurance company. Her six-year-old son, Christian, follows her out of the door and scrambles into the white Ford Escort which stands in the garage. Liane drives Christian to his school in the village, then sets out across the Derbyshire hills towards Liverpool.

She has three appointments in Ellesmere Port today. First, a fertilizer factory, then Ince B power station, and finally the Shell petrochemical refinery. At each plant she will be meeting instrument engineers and trying to persuade them to buy a particular brand of electronic instruments.

Liane is a sales representative for Measurement Technology Ltd, a small and relatively new engineering firm based in Luton. She is the only rep they have on the road and her job covers nine counties in the north of England.

Her career with MTL began three years ago when she was hired as an assistant to the Production Director. At the time she lived near Luton. Barry was working in London and Christian, then three years old, went to a day nursery. Liane spent most of her time working as a records clerk, filing information about the company's stock. She also helped out in the buying department. MTL was expanding. Soon the Production Director was too busy to handle the buying department, so Liane took over that side of his job. She ordered all the components and materials needed to build MTL's equipment – semi-conductors, diodes, resistors, metal casing, wire, nuts, bolts, glue . . . And as she did so she learnt how the instruments were made, what they did and how they worked. The job suited her well. The company went on expanding and soon Liane had an assistant of her own.

After two years Barry was promoted and transferred to Sheffield. Liane handed in her notice. The directors were sorry to see her go – she was hard-working, competent and loyal. They suggested that she might like to become their first sales representative, working from her new home in the north. They put her on a three-month trial.

At first Liane hated her new job. She didn't know the territory and kept getting lost on the roads. Before the company gave her a car she had to drive her own Fiat 500 which was noisy, slow and uncomfortable on long trips. She had to travel almost 200 miles a day, meet total strangers and carry out a job for which she had neither training nor experience. Winter came and the roads were treacherous. Once it took her seven hours to get home from Bradford, a distance of 39 miles. But now that she has a better car, knows the roads and is more familiar with her job, she loves it. MTL are happy; they confirmed her appointment after only two months.

Liane was given a dossier of possible customers in the nine counties. It listed manufacturing companies that were likely to need the sort of instruments MTL produced, with the names of engineers responsible for ordering them. She was told to go through the list and visit as many of the companies as possible. She makes appointments by telephone first. She doesn't sell goods on the spot, nor does she take orders. Her job is to update and expand the list of customers, to contact the appropriate people and to find out about current and future projects which may require MTL's equipment. She relays this information to headquarters and arranges for catalogues and samples to be sent where needed. If the engineers raise any questions she can't answer she refers them to the technical department at Luton, but in fact she has a fairly thorough knowledge of MTL's range of equipment and deals with most of the queries herself.

The company's most successful products are 'intrinsic safety barriers' for use in hazardous industrial zones. Liane explained as she drove towards Ellesmere Port: 'Some manufacturing processes are highly dangerous because they involve chemicals or gases that are explosive or inflammable. All processes need instruments to measure and control them. Most instruments nowadays are electronic – they use an electric current which can produce a spark. A single spark can cause an explosion in a hazardous area by igniting the gases or chemicals. So a barrier has to be created between the instruments and the hazardous zone. MTL has designed a special barrier for this purpose. We also make a range of transmitters, trip amplifiers, millivolt converters . . .' As we continued on our way, she explained in some detail how each of these worked.

She wishes she had trained as an engineer, but has no technical qualifications. She was born and brought up in West Germany in the northern port of Bremen. Her father works in the sales department of a spinning machine factory and her mother is a cashier in a supermarket. When Liane was 15, one of her neighbours became pregnant – an 18-year-old girl who was unmarried and halfway through her apprenticeship to qualify as a draughtswoman. She gave up her training, married the father and had the baby. Because of this cautionary example, Liane's parents feared the same fate would befall their own daughter, and planned her education accordingly.

They had already decided that it would be a waste of time to send her to university (although she was bright enough and her teachers encouraged her) because they felt so convinced that she would marry at an early age and drop any studies. Now, they also determined that she should not enter into an apprenticeship in case she too became pregnant and wasted years of training. So they sent her to a commercial school where she was taught to be a secretary. Her first job was in the typing pool of a large shipping company in Bremen. She loathed it.

Liane is neither specially ambitious, nor exceptionally clever, but she has a strong sense of her own worth and confidence enough to convey this to others. Before long she had persuaded her employer to move her out of the typing pool and into the office of the two men for whom she had been typing. She found out more about their work. One of them left and she stepped into his job. Ships from all over the world came into dry dock for repair. Liane had to prepare invoices in English with details and prices of every item involved in the repair. It was better than typing. The experience she gained there led MTL to employ her three years later. But after a year and a half she'd had enough of it. Her wages were low. She was 19 and she wanted an adventure, so she decided to come to England. As soon as she quit, the company advertised for a man to do her job at twice the salary.

She made her way to Cheltenham in Gloucestershire where she worked as an au pair for the wife of a wealthy businessman. It was typical of many au pair jobs – she worked much harder than she should have done while the lady of the house complained that she ate too much and was too expensive to keep. At the end of that year she met Barry at a Christmas party. By the middle of the next year she had married him. 'I had no intention of getting married so soon, but when I tried to get another job in England – even a typing job, I was prepared to do anything – it was impossible because I didn't have a work permit. So Barry said "I'll marry you," and I said, "Thank you very much!"' She got pregnant on honeymoon. And, as her parents had predicted, she was a wife and mother by the time she was 21.

When Christian was old enough to go to a nursery, she went to work for MTL. Her parents had not foretold that she would be a travelling sales rep by the age of 26.

The job fits in well with her domestic responsibilities. She goes out on the road three days a week and works at home the rest of the time. She can take extra unpaid holidays when she needs them. A neighbour who has four children of her own looks after Christian when he is not at school. Barry helps to do the cleaning but Liane assumes responsibility for most of the housework. Unlike other travelling reps, she has to go home every evening to feed her family.

Once she had to stay overnight in a hotel in Middlesbrough and spent some time at the bar, drinking and talking with the other reps. At the end of the evening she had to fight off their amorous advances, then endure some unfriendly repartee as they nursed their bruised egos over breakfast.

But that's the only troublesome incident she has encountered. She is not self-conscious about her looks, nor is she distrustful of the opposite sex. If she had a different outlook, she might find her job less tolerable.

After driving for two and a half hours, she arrives at Ellesmere Port and parks in front of the APU fertilizer factory. She checks the contents of her briefcase, combs her hair, takes two rectangular gadgets out of the boot. The receptionist directs her upstairs to Mr Hooper's office. A man in his early thirties, his face rather pink beneath a receding hairline, shakes her hand and offers her a chair. Liane finds the men she meets in the course of her work often seem slightly nervous. Mr Hooper is not at all sure how to treat her. The women he knows at work are either secretaries, clerks or tea ladies. He knows how to deal with them. But here is a woman selling electronic instruments. Can she be serious? She is young, beautiful and her hair is blonde. Surely she can't know much about measurement technology? Is she just an attractive lure? And if so, how is *he* supposed to behave? He daren't look her in the eye.

All the same, he is glad to meet her. This is the most interesting thing that has happened at the office for some time. He hurries away to make cups of coffee. When he returns they exchange a few pleasantries about the weather, a few generalities about the company. Then they begin to discuss MTL's range of equipment. Liane goes through the brochure with Mr Hooper, pointing out items she thinks may interest him. She shows him the samples she has brought from the car. Gradually, he relaxes. And once engrossed in his own subject he abandons the jocular, patronizing manner with which he has been trying to hide his confusion. Liane continues, charming and businesslike. She knows what she is talking about, she understands his questions, she provides him with some useful information and takes a keen interest in a new project he is planning. In fact, she behaves just like any good sales representative. But Mr Hooper will probably remember her when the other reps are forgotten.

Ince B is the next stop – the vast construction site of a new oil-fired power station. Here, the offices are not yet built and the engineers are working in huts. Liane arrives at the wrong door, to be met by a group of construction workers. They are convulsed with nudging and winking and ask if she has come to give them a strip-tease. When eventually they direct her to the makeshift offices, she is followed by a chorus of catcalls, whistles and merry suggestions dressed in varying degrees of obscenity. Liane is unperturbed. (I am cringing, trying to hide behind her.)

The engineer she is due to meet is not available, so instead she sees his deputy, a tall young man in voluminous dungarees and a tin helmet. He is courteous, serious, but seems at a bit of a loss. What kind of a discussion can he have with a non-technical sales rep? Liane begins to question him about the Ince B construction programme, reminds him that MTL's transmitters have been approved by the Central Electricity Generating Board, describes the advantages of a particular type of amplifier. 'Blimey, you know more than I do,' he murmurs, adjusting the level of his conversation. 'Can these temperature transmitters be used in Zone 2? What are the safety requirements . . . ?'

On her last call of the day, Liane meets Mr Stanley and Mr Mack. Their office is right out in the middle of the huge network of pipes and tanks at the Shell refinery. Both men already know something about MTL's equipment. Mr Mack is comradely. Mr Stanley is guarded. 'MTL barriers are a confounded nuisance. They don't fit on the bus bars.' Liane assures him that they do. He doesn't believe her. Patiently, she explains. He concedes. She shows him a new MTL barrier which can feed a higher current into the hazardous area. He is impressed. Mr Mack is interested in temperature transmitters. Liane points out that one of MTL's transmitters can be adjusted on site for use with different thermocouples, and adds that MTL has a wider range and makes faster deliveries than its main competitor in the field. He is enthusiastic. 'Excellent, smashing service!'

Her work over, Liane heads back to Sheffield. She rates it a good average day. There's a strong chance of big orders from APU in two or three years, if Mr Hooper's project goes through. Next time they're buying equipment at Ince B, they're more likely to remember MTL instead of automatically placing orders with its competitors. And the people at Shell seemed to take a genuine interest in several products.

She arrives home at 6.30. As usual, Barry has collected Christian from school. Now he is sitting in the garden with two of their friends who have dropped by for a drink. Liane asks them to stay for supper. They protest – she must be tired. She insists. They agree. And she disappears into the kitchen to prepare a salad.

Jocelyn Burnell

Astronomer

Thousands of children, generation after generation, have been fascinated by the stars and the mysteries of outer space. Jocelyn was no exception. What marks her out from the rest is that she has managed to translate her childhood fascination into a career. She gives Mr Tillott much of the credit for that.

Brought up in a Quaker family in Northern Ireland, she was sent to England at the age of 13 to attend a Quaker school in York. Mr Tillott was the physics master. 'He'd come out of retirement to teach us and he was excellent. The school wasn't well equipped for science. He used to open a catalogue, show us a picture and say: "*That's* a tangent galvanometer", or whatever he was talking about at the time, and then he'd say: "Look at the price!" Nevertheless, he was such a good teacher that he made me realize physics was something I could do quite easily. He got me hooked on it.'

Jocelyn took A-levels in physics and maths and went to Glasgow university to do a degree in physics. 'I wanted to do astronomy but at the last minute decided it was unwise. If you want to be an astronomer you've got to be sufficiently bright to stay on at university to do research. At that stage I wasn't sure if I was bright enough to make the grade.'

At Glasgow, she became increasingly single-minded about astronomy, especially radio astronomy. This is a relatively new branch of the science which involves recording and analysing radio waves produced by stars, most of which are invisible to the human eye, even through the most sophisticated optical telescope.

It turned out she *was* bright enough: she got a good second-class degree, and when she applied to do a Ph.D. in astronomy she was given a place at Cambridge. Her supervisor was a man called Tony Hewish, who later won a Nobel prize. She went to work at the Radio Astronomy Observatory six miles outside Cambridge and spent most of the next two years doing manual labour in a nearby field.

'My supervisor had designed a new telescope for measuring radio waves and he was ready to start building it when I arrived. It was a great big aerial which looked like a hop field – lots of wooden posts with wires strung between them. The work was extremely energetic and sometimes desperately monotonous – sledge-hammering, putting plugs on cables, things like that.' Her reward came in the third year when the radio telescope was complete and she was given the job of operating it.

'There were cables leading from the aerial in the field to a radio receiver in the lab. Instead of producing sound, this receiver produced a tracing on a chart: the radio signals were used to drive a pen. I had to analyse these chart recordings, check through them and take measurements. We were meant to be looking for a particular type of radio source known as a "quasar". This is an object like a galaxy which is believed to be very distant, miles beyond our own galaxy, right away near the edge of the visible universe. The telescope was designed to make a survey of these quasars, so that we could pick them out and catalogue them.' Jocelyn was preparing a thesis on quasars, entitled 'The Measurement of Angular Diameters of Radio Sources by a Diffraction Method'. But quasars and thesis were soon overshadowed by more intriguing events.

'The telescope was picking up a signal which we didn't understand. It didn't look like a quasar and it didn't look like man-made interference. We nick-named it the scruff. It turned out to be an incredible new type of star.' That was how Jocelyn made one of the most important astronomical finds of the century.

There was no instant flash of recognition, no leaping around the laboratory with shouts of 'Eureka!' It took Jocelyn weeks of diligent searching through charts and careful testing. 'When you observe something that seems rather odd, you try to think of experiments you can do to test its various properties. Astronomy's rather a frustrating subject because you can't go up to a star and twiddle a knob to make it behave differently. In almost any other branch of science you can alter the thing you are looking at. But with a star you can only observe the radiation it sends to earth. Anyway, we tried out various ideas. Whatever it was, it was sending out a flash. Stars that flash are a bit peculiar, but stars that flash once a second are really incredible. We just couldn't believe it *was* a star, so we tested the theory that it was another civilization signalling to us. We argued that if the signal was produced by "little green men", they'd be on a planet, their "earth", going round a star, their "sun". If this was the case, they'd be coming towards us some of the time, the flashes would start to pile up on each other, and the gap between them would get shorter. The reverse would happen as they circled back again. So we timed the flashes very accurately over a couple of months. It kept on flashing at regular one-second intervals.'

They enlisted two other astronomers at the Observatory to trace the signals on a second telescope, to make sure they weren't caused by a fault in their equipment. Gradually, they were able to dismiss more and more of their theories. Then Jocelyn discovered three identical radio sources in other parts of the sky. There were no more alternative explanations left. They had to conclude that it was indeed a new – and extraordinary – type of star. 'Compared with quasars, these stars are virtually on our doorstep. They're beyond our solar system but well within our galaxy. They're very small and very heavy. A typical star might measure a million miles across. These measure only ten miles, yet they weigh as much as an ordinary star – a thousand million million million million tons, all crammed into a sphere ten miles across! Apparently they're spinning. And they produce a radio wave like a lighthouse beam. So we get this flash every time the beam spins round past us.'

In February 1968, Tony Hewish announced the discovery at a special seminar in Cambridge. They called the new stars 'pulsars' because of their pulse-like flash. Jocelyn had been so absorbed in her efforts to explain them away as something less bizarre that she only began to sense the excitement of the event when she saw how other astronomers were reacting. One of them rushed out of the seminar to phone New York. The curious signals she had detected three months earlier became an international sensation overnight.

In the midst of all this, Jocelyn got engaged to an under-graduate called Martin Burnell, whom she had met at a Quaker gathering in Cambridge. When she had finished her thesis, adding the pulsars as an appendix, she got married and moved to the south coast near Chichester, Sussex, where Martin had a job as a trainee in local government.

'If I hadn't married I'd have done my level best to stay in Cambridge. Of all the branches of astronomy, radio was my first love. But at the time I wasn't very sure about how keen I was to keep on working. I thought I might be quite happy as a housewife. I would advise anyone else who finds herself in a similar situation to keep all her options open. I soon discovered that I *did* want to work – and then I had the nasty problem of finding a job within commuting distance of Chichester.' The nearest astronomy laboratories were 20 miles away at Southampton university, so for five years Jocelyn travelled 40 miles a day and hopped uneasily from one temporary fellowship to another, learning about gamma ray astronomy, doing some teaching and generally feeling she was not achieving a great deal.

She left Southampton when her son Gavin was born. Just at that time Martin got a new job which meant they had to move to Horsham in the north of Sussex. 'Again, I fondly imagined I would be prepared to stay at home and be a housewife and mother. After a few weeks I knew I'd made a mistake. I was going batty! I hadn't realized how much stimulation I got from my work, even when it wasn't terribly successful. I was bored at home – I'm not terribly interested in small babies.'

Almost subconsciously, she had prepared an escape route. When Martin applied for the job in Horsham, she checked out that there was another space laboratory within reach of the town. She made some tentative enquiries there and found that they were keen to employ her. When Gavin was nine months old, she set about finding a childminder and then went to work part-time as an Associate Research Fellow at the Mullard Space Science Laboratories.

Three days a week she rides a round trip of 25 miles on her motor scooter to Holmbury House, a large mansion in the Surrey hills with a spectacular view over open fields to the south. What was once a rather splendid stately home now has computer terminals tucked under the grand staircase and tons of elaborate experimental equipment in the west drawing room. The property of University College London, it is utilized (more constructively than in its past life, no doubt) by many earnest young astronomers. There's an intense intellectual comradeship among them and the fact that Jocelyn is the only woman appears to make no difference at all to the way her colleagues treat her.

'I was taken on as a computer programmer and I expected it to be terribly routine. But it's been pandemonium! I didn't believe I could have such good luck twice in my life.'

This time she is working in yet another branch of astronomy, studying x-ray signals from space.* 'X-ray astronomy is quite difficult because you can't do it from the ground. The earth's atmosphere cuts out all the x-rays which would otherwise reach us from the stars, so you have to put your x-ray telescope on to a satellite or a rocket or a high altitude balloon. Rocket flights only last about five minutes and balloon flights last eight hours if you're lucky. Until you get a satellite up there, the amount of data you can collect is very limited. Ours was launched in 1974 from a platform off the coast of Kenya and it's circling the Equator at a height of about 500 kilometres. It was one of the first to go up with an x-ray telescope on board and there's a tremendous harvest of data to be reaped. We've discovered new kinds of x-ray sources, x-ray stars behaving in ways we hadn't expected – all sorts of fascinating things.'

Just as radio astronomy was coming of age when Jocelyn arrived at Cambridge, so x-ray astronomy began to 'boom' with the first of the signals from the satellite, about six months after she started work at Holmbury House. It turned out that x-ray stars were the same type of small, dense 'neutron' star as the pulsars; some of them even flashed. Inevitably Jocelyn with her special experience was pulled in to help analyse the data.

It has emerged as a further source of excitement that x-ray astronomy is probably the only way to observe the notorious 'black holes' (if it is eventually established that they really do exist). According to the theory, black holes were once stars until they ran out of fuel, at which point they began to shrink under the force of their own gravity. 'It's not yet proven that they *do* exist,'

*If you're confused about the different types of radiation to which Jocelyn refers, I couldn't offer you a clearer explanation than her own:
'You've seen a rainbow with its various colours: red, orange, yellow, green, blue, indigo, violet. (At school we were taught to remember it by the jingle Rowntrees Of York Give Best In Value – a superb bit of indoctrination!) These colours are the parts of the spectrum that the human eye can see. Each one is a similar type of ray, but with a different wave-length. Beyond the red of the spectrum there are more wave-lengths which we can't see because they're too long for the human eye to detect. The first is infra-red, as in infra-red lamps. Then there's microwave, as in microwave ovens. Beyond microwave there are radio waves – a whole range of wave-lengths and channels you can tune your radio to, rather like tuning to different colours. In radio astronomy we pick up not BBC broadcasts but radio signals which arise perfectly naturally in stars, galaxies and clouds of gas out in space. Now, if you go back to the other side of the spectrum, beyond violet, you come to ultra-violet. On this side the wave-lengths are too short for the human eye to detect. Beyond ultra-violet there are x-rays. Some stars and clouds of gas produce x-rays instead of radio waves. Beyond x-rays there are gamma rays.'

says Jocelyn, true scientist that she is. 'But we believe that if a star were very heavy, say 20 times the size of the sun, its gravity could be so strong that when it began to shrink its inherent strength would be unable to withstand the force of its gravity. So we may be faced with the lovely situation of a whole star, weighing thousands of millions of millions of millions of millions of tons, shrinking to zero radius. A point in the universe with incredibly strong gravity, it would pull things into it but would not let anything out – no light or radiation. The only way we would be able to detect it would be by observing material just before it was swallowed up, because the material would get quite hot and uncomfortable and emit x-rays.

'We've been studying one x-ray source which could indicate a black hole. Quite a lot of stars are in pairs, orbiting round each other, and this one looks as if it could be a star orbiting round a black hole, sending out x-rays. There are still some alternative explanations but they are getting less plausible as time goes past and we may soon be forced to admit that the theory is correct.'

So much for the routine little job she rode off to four years ago. Jocelyn insists that she has been exceptionally lucky. Generally, astronomy is far less dramatic – indeed, the chief attraction for astronomers is not the possibility of sensational discoveries, but the close scrutiny of data, the building, testing and demolition of theories, the gradual inching out of the borders of knowledge.

Jocelyn is keen to go on working at Holmbury House for as long as possible, but she's resigned to the fact that her job there can't last. 'Martin won't want to stay at Horsham forever. In his line of work the only way to get on is by moving from one borough to another. He may find something within reach of this laboratory, but he's quite senior now and there aren't all that many suitable openings for someone in his position. Each time Martin thinks about moving, we look very carefully to see what there might be for me in the area. If I can't get a job in astronomy I suppose I could work in industry, computer programming or something like that.' She didn't sound too keen on the idea. 'One great advantage of this job is that it's so flexible. As long as I put in the hours, no one minds when I do them. I imagine it would be impossible to find a job as flexible as this outside the universities.'

The Burnells live in a three-bedroomed detached house in a smart modern estate on the outskirts of Horsham. Jocelyn is almost unique among her female neighbours in having a small child *and* a job. She finds herself a little out of key with the women on the estate as most are full-time housewives with two or more children and no prospect of going out to work.

'I don't think I shall have any more children. If I do, I'll try very hard to keep on working. But it won't be easy. Even with one child I find it physically very tough coping with a house and child as well as a job. When Martin and I got married, we both thought we'd divide the housework evenly between us. In fact, we'd underestimated how much we'd both been socially conditioned. When it comes to the crunch, when it's ten at night and the washing up still hasn't been done, it's *me* who has a guilty conscience rather than Martin. There are still tremendous pressures on us to conform to the traditional male and female roles. Martin has an extremely demanding job and he's usually clapped-out when he comes home. I think male career patterns are still based on the assumption that there's a wife at home as a full-time support. It's been harder to insist that he shares the work since we had a child and I stopped working full-time. It has meant that I've burnt my boats, destroyed the chance of equality at home. I can't really complain now if Martin doesn't do a half-share of the housework.'

On Tuesdays and Thursdays, Gavin – now a lively four-year-old, showing no sign whatever of maternal (or paternal) deprivation – goes to a morning playgroup instead of to the childminder. Jocelyn stays away from the laboratory, does her shopping and housework during the morning and looks after him at home in the afternoon.

'Now that he's approaching five, I'm interested to see how his attitude to male and female roles is developing. I've been horrified to hear comments like "Daddy, you and I'll go and play in the garden while Mummy does the washing up." Where does he get *that* from? It certainly isn't from me!

'He's beginning to take an interest in the fact that I work, that I look at the stars. I've had some difficulty explaining to him that although I'm an astronomer I don't use an ordinary telescope, but a satellite instead. I think he's got the hang of it now, but he has a pretty rough ride sometimes. He goes off to his playgroup and when someone says: "What does your Mummy do, Gavin?" he'll answer: "My Mummy looks after a satellite." Well who's going to believe *that*?'

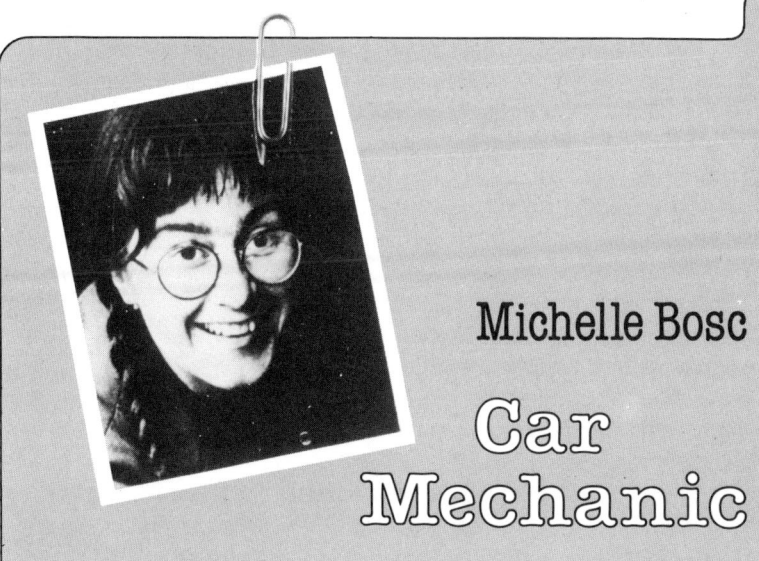

Michelle Bosc

Car Mechanic

When Michelle was at school her friends and teachers would never have guessed how she'd turn out. The only daughter of a postman and a telephonist, she grew up in a small village near Lyons in France. She was a conventional, obedient child who worked hard and won a place at Bordeaux university to study Humanities (literature, history and philosophy). Her parents were delighted that she was to have the educational opportunities they had missed. They hoped she would be a school teacher. But things didn't happen quite as they had wished.

Michelle's great ambition was to travel. She wanted to be a journalist – until she discovered that real journalists seldom travelled beyond the doorsteps of their own town. When she finished her course at Bordeaux she joined a theatre group as an administrator, toured with them through Europe and ended up in London. By that time she had decided not to pursue an intellectual career. But she had no idea what to do instead. She worked as a model for the students at Hammersmith Art College and joined the women's movement. It was really only by accident that she developed an interest in mechanics.

She got a job as a printer's clerk with the charity Christian Action, helping to operate a small litho press. 'I enjoyed the process of the machine. I loved the rumbling noise it made. I even liked getting covered with ink and oil. I suppose it fitted in with an image I have of myself. I like to think I am a bit tough. So, if I'm dirty, it helps!'

71

At about this time she passed her driving test and bought herself an ancient Ford Popular. The car was her pride and joy — and a constant source of anxiety. 'I worried about every little thing. If there was a noise I hadn't heard before, I had to open the bonnet. If an indicator wasn't working I couldn't stop myself fiddling about to see if I could fix it.

'One day I tried to start the car and there was an *awful* noise. I looked underneath and there was this great big lump of metal hanging down under the engine. I have a friend who's a mechanic. He came round the next day to have a look. He laughed a lot when he saw what had happened. The nuts that hold the starter motor in place had come loose and it had fallen down. He fixed it in five minutes and I had been worrying all night about it. Well — I envied that sort of person!'

Next time something went wrong with her car, Michelle watched her friend as he mended it. He showed her how two small screws on the carburretor could be adjusted to tune it. If you moved them a fraction of an inch either way, they would alter the speed of the engine and make it run more smoothly. 'If the car starts stalling,' he told her, 'try turning *this* one.'

Soon afterwards she drove up to Scotland with a friend. By the time they reached Edinburgh the car was stalling at every traffic light. Michelle took it into a garage. 'When I collected it I noticed the engine was revving very fast all the time. This didn't seem right so I drove into another garage and asked for a screwdriver. Then — my big discovery! When I looked inside the carburretor I saw that all they had done was to set the choke so that it was always on. This stopped the car from stalling but made it run on a very rich mixture, which was why the revs were so high. I put the choke back to normal, then I balanced those two little screws until the engine sounded right. The car didn't stall again.'

For Michelle (as for most girls) mechanical things had always been cloaked in mystery — so this was a triumph. Her passion for the old Ford grew as she became more confident in diagnosing its ailments. When she heard about the Government TOPS* scheme which would pay her a grant while she learnt a new skill, two courses attracted her: one was typing, the other was car maintenance and repair. She enquired at the Employment Exchange. 'The man at the desk said yes, it would be fine for me to apply for the typing course. He brushed aside my query about car mechanics as if he hadn't heard.' Michelle filed away the idea and went off

*See pp. 92–3 for further information on TOPS

on her own to hitch-hike around north-west Africa. In Algiers she made friends with a student named Ali and stayed several months. Eventually she came back to London, glad to be home, but restless.

It was Jeannie who finally prompted her to train as a mechanic. Jeannie had just moved into a room in Michelle's flat and she herself had applied for a Government training course in carpentry. Michelle put in her application and the two women waited on tenterhooks to see if they'd be called for interviews. 'We were sure they'd try to put us off, and ask awkward questions about why we were interested in learning these skills.'

They spent days rehearsing questions and answers, but it turned out that the Government Skill Centre was glad to take them on. Michelle had to answer a few basic questions about cars, such as: 'What is a differential?' and 'How do you tune a carburettor?' She answered satisfactorily and was told she could start the course. 'The next six months were the happiest in my life. It's true – I was glad to get up at 6.30 in the morning to go to the Skill Centre. I was unhappy on Fridays when the week was over and I hated the weekends.'

In the first week the 12 students were given a metal chipping exercise to complete. They were told to change a cylindrical shape into a rectangle by chiselling and filing. It had to be right to 1000th of an inch. 'It was an exercise in patience. They wanted to see how we would react. It was also very hard work. I got blisters on my hands, cramp in my shoulder, aches in my arm. But I didn't care, it was such a revelation to find I could make different shapes with metal.'

Most of the men on the course had done metal work before, either at school or in previous jobs. 'They kept offering to help me. "That's not right, love," they'd say, "let me show you". I probably was quite clumsy but I had to insist on doing it myself.'

For 13 weeks, the students were taught the basic skills and procedures of car mechanics. After that they did maintenance and repair of customers' cars, under supervision. Their training was predominantly practical, with one two-hour lecture a week which dealt with theory.

'The course was very well conceived. The instructor was an excellent mechanic. He was also open-minded and he seemed to understand why I was there. He took me seriously. It was important to me that the men could see that women were able to do a job like that, so I was very conscientious and I used to check everything I did at least three times. I had to convince them I wasn't just playing.'

The male students liked Michelle and treated her well, but they seemed to have difficulty in sharing work with her. She noticed the instructor kept giving her jobs on her own, while the men usually worked in twos or threes. 'I told him I felt isolated. If I was going to work in a garage I would have to learn to work with other people. After that he started putting me to work in the teams. This created a curious situation. The men would get worried and very competitive – as if they were afraid I would be better than them. I tried to talk to them about it, but I don't think they understood what I was getting at. After a while I had to go back and admit I was happier working on my own.'

Michelle is such a gentle, diffident creature it would be wrong to imagine that she was overbearing towards her fellow students. She has a warm, open manner, a lovely dimpled smile and an enchanting French accent. She is entirely at ease with herself, yet still full of doubts about her abilities as a mechanic. She worries, takes copious notes of new things to learn and reflects carefully upon every job she does.

Her first really heavy task was to change a wheel on a three-ton lorry. (Next time you see a lorry consider the weight of a single wheel.) 'You have to sit down with your legs out in front of you. When you've removed all the nuts you lift your knees up so that your legs take part of the weight as the wheel comes off. Then you roll it sideways across your thighs, on to the ground. Once you know how it's quite easy.

'Physical effort is not an obstacle. There were men on the course who were just as small as me. If you can't handle something on your own, there's usually a way round it. I learnt very quickly to use leverage and cranes and jacks.

'I remember the first clutch I changed on my own. It was in a Ford Cortina. To change a clutch you have to remove the gearbox and the Cortina gearbox is very big and heavy. First you disconnect everything from above, then you have to lie down under the car and remove the bolts which hold it in place. Then you lift it down with your arms and legs. If you're not careful it can fall on you. Putting it back is even harder. You have to lift it up and jiggle it about until it fits into place. There's usually something in the way. An experienced mechanic can do the job in less than six hours. It took me a day and a half, but I can do it in half a day now.'

One day Michelle was called in to see the supervisor. He wanted to tell her she had done particularly well; of all the students she had made the most progress.

When the course came to an end the training officer attached to the Skill Centre found three garages willing to interview Michelle. It hadn't been easy. Several garages had refused point-blank even to consider hiring a woman.* However, the three that did interview Michelle all offered her a job. She choose a BMW garage in west London. It wasn't a lucky choice.

'There are four other mechanics. One of them is quite friendly when he's in a good mood, but the others are very dour. There are days when no one says anything to me except: "Can I borrow a spanner?" or "Hurry up with that car". One of them makes really hostile jokes about women whenever I am around. There used to be a young guy called Geoff who was nice, but he got so fed up with the others that he left.'

*This was just before the Sex Discrimination Act of 1975

'The pay is poor. I'm the only one in a union – the others aren't interested. We work a nine-hour day with two tea breaks and no lunch hour. I get really exhausted. Sometimes when I come home at night, all I can do is go straight to bed. I think it's worse because I have no friendly support at work. It could be much easier if I had someone sympathetic to talk to. All the time I feel as if I'm in the middle of the jungle.'

Apparently Michelle's employers appreciate her (though they don't use money to show it). They sent her on a one-week BMW training course shortly after she joined and since then have expected her to service and repair cars on her own, which is unusual for someone with so little experience. There were a dozen mechanics on the course. The 11 men, who came from BMW garages all over the country, seemed to resent Michelle's presence. They jeered whenever she asked questions and delivered jocular warnings about what 11 men could do to one woman when the instructor left the room. They all took a test at the end of the week and Michelle came top with 94 per cent.

The garage in which she works is a small outfit with room for working on five or six cars at a time. It's well-lit and well-equipped. The atmosphere was relatively cheerful when I went there, largely because Geoff had returned (temporarily) and was working on the car next to Michelle's, to her obvious relief. He dislikes the atmosphere even more than she does, but at least they can joke about it. 'What I can't stand about this place, Michelle,' says Geoff, raising his eyes to heaven, 'is the noise, the laughter, the singing. I wish they'd all simmer down.'

That morning the foreman, a large humourless fellow, had told Michelle she was working too slowly. 'But that's because I'm still learning,' she protested. 'I'm paid less than you because I work more slowly.'

'If you want more money ask the manager,' he retorted brusquely, missing the point.

At the end of the day Michelle drove home in her 17-year-old Austin Cambridge (the Popular had given up the ghost). She had paid £60 for this car. The other day she'd jacked it up in the road and put a new clutch in it. She reckoned the car still had a long life ahead of it.

Back at her flat, she cooked a magnificent omelette for Jeannie and me. Jeannie was now working as a carpenter for Camden Borough Council, renovating old houses. She loved her job. We discussed Michelle's dilemma. Her pay and conditions were bad, but was it too soon for her to leave? She'd been there only five months. She was still totally committed to working as a mechanic and she was learning a lot from BMW who had promised to send her on another training course soon. How could she be sure that it would be any better at the next garage? Her best bet might be to get into a bigger garage where the mechanics were properly unionized. Perhaps she could train as a bus mechanic with London Transport . . .

Michelle has no wish to marry or have children. She still writes to her friend Ali and he is the only man she would want to share a home with. But it would be hard for him to leave Algiers and Michelle feels she belongs in England now. Besides, a Muslim country like Algeria, where women are still veiled and kept in purdah, would not be the easiest place for her to find work as a mechanic!

'When I have had two or three more years' experience, I would like to open a garage of my own. I would really love to have a women's garage. I could take on girl apprentices because I know how hard it can be for a girl to train with men. All my customers could be women – because women so often get a bad deal from garages. Nobody explains to them what is wrong with their cars and they get ripped off because they don't know what's going on.'

It's ironic that Michelle cannot open a women's garage without contravening the Sex Discrimination Act. But she could no doubt find a way round the law if she wanted to. Private clubs are exempt. Perhaps she will found the first Women's Car Maintenance and Repair Club.

Sue Kibble
Sue Field

Two Accountants

Sue Kibble

In an elegant cul-de-sac behind Parliament Square, a tall Queen Anne residence is now the headquarters of Associated Fisheries, a consortium of fishing and food processing companies with an annual turnover of around £100 million. Sue Kibble turns up for work on a bicycle, wearing jeans and a scarlet anorak. By tradition female clerical staff are expected to wear skirts and male executives to wear suits and ties. But no one minds what Sue wears as there are no conventions for someone as rare as a female accountant.

Her office is on the top floor with a fine view of St James's park. It is a bare, functional room with two large desks, four filing cabinets and bookshelves piled haphazardly with files and ledgers and reference books. On Sue's desk there is an electric adding machine, a pocket calculator, a telephone, a heap of papers and a large analysis ledger into which she is copying scores of columns of figures by hand.

The cashier put his head round the door. 'I rang the bank. No joy. All they said was that they may have made "alternative arrangements".'

'Oh crikey!' Sue had been waiting for this news. She grabbed the telephone and dialled the Group's solicitors. 'Good morning, I've just heard from the bank,' (no need to announce herself, apparently): 'we've been assured it's a rubber cheque. I think the next enquiry had better come from you . . .'

A cheque made out to Associated Fisheries had bounced for the second time. A fairly substantial sum was involved. Sue had to tell the Group's solicitors to take whatever steps were necessary to recover the money. Then she rushed out of her office to inform the relevant director.

She told me she spent a lot of her time chasing round trying to sort out little dramas of one kind or another. Now she will have to calculate the sum as a possible loss in the Group's annual accounts. She went on pencilling numbers into the tiny squares in the ledger.

She is Assistant to the Chief Accountant at Associated Fisheries. Some people would hate her job – endless figures, detailed calculations, checking and re-checking, dry financial abstractions; but it suits her. She is interested in business, in profits and losses, in management and all things financial. She finds great satisfaction in imposing order on all those figures. She enjoys dealing with solicitors and other accountants, directors and bank managers, and meeting people at all levels of business. She imposes her own cheerfully informal style on everything she does and takes home what most women would consider to be a fairly hefty salary.

She was brought up in Weybridge, Surrey. Her father is a solicitor, her mother an accountant. 'As a child I used to spend hours helping her cross-check balances to agree her accounts for the office.' When Sue left school at 16 she was sent to a vocational guidance agency – a private organization which sets its clients aptitude tests and then directs them to 'suitable' jobs in return for a fee. She had thought of following in her father's footsteps, but the agency told her the training wouldn't suit her and advised her to follow her mother's example instead. She thinks they were probably right. She took her articles* with a Guildford firm of chartered accountants and lived at home, studying for her exams in the evenings, while most of her girl friends went off to London to be secretaries.

She learnt how to prepare accurate records of money spent and received; how to book-keep; how to work out budgets which estimate how much money will be spent and received in future; how to chart the flow of cash and estimate the value of goods; how to work out interest on debts and loans; how to prepare accounts for the Inland Revenue and anticipate the amount of tax that will have to be paid on profits. She also learnt to check financial records prepared by other people – a process known as

*Practical training, see p. 126

auditing. All limited companies are obliged by law to have their accounts audited by independent professional accountants before they are presented to the Inland Revenue and (in the case of public companies) to their shareholders.

'I used to go out on audits with the senior accountants. We'd visit all sorts of people, not just businessmen, but local farms and golf clubs and charities like the Surrey Red Cross. We even handled accounts for the Women's Institute.' Sue qualified after five years' articles, then moved to Midgeley Snelling, a firm of chartered accountants in London.

Here, as in Guildford, she worked for a variety of clients, although now the majority were conventional businesses. For some larger companies she audited accounts prepared by their own staff. For others, she worked out how much tax they would have to pay. And for some smaller businesses she prepared their annual accounts for presentation to the Inland Revenue and to let proprietors know how much net profit they had made in the year.

She liked the work but after two years decided it was taking up too much of her life. She signed on with an agency to do temporary work. 'I worked for a film director and was shown round Pinewood Studios. I worked for a wig company – wigs were all the rage then – and it was quite an exciting job as I was closely involved in running the business. Then one day my old firm rang up and asked if I wanted to work in Bermuda for six months. The job was just auditing which I found rather slow after commercial life, but otherwise I had a lovely time out there.'

Shortly after she came back she married Robert Kibble whom she had met at Midgeley Snelling where he was an articled clerk. When she got back from honeymoon she started work at Associated Fisheries.

Qualified accountants are usually employed in one of two capacities. Some work as independent chartered accountants, usually grouped together in partnerships like those at Midgeley Snelling. They have lots of different clients, for whom they prepare accounts, carry out audits, estimate taxation or give financial advice. Others are employed full-time by an organization – just as Sue is now employed by Associated Fisheries – to prepare their accounts and help manage their financial affairs. 'As an independent chartered accountant you're usually dealing with last year's accounts, you're an onlooker asking awkward questions. In commerce you're more involved in the action behind the figures, you're dealing with things that are happening *now*. The more senior you get, the more interesting the work becomes. You're not just doing routine checking; you have to deal with queries, advise directors, supervise other people's work. You become more and more involved in the management of the company.'

The biggest part of Sue's job is preparing for publication the annual consolidated accounts of Associated Fisheries. There are approximately 75 subsidiary companies each of which has accountants who draw up their own separate accounts. (Sue does them for the Head Office in London.) Each set of accounts is separately audited by independent chartered accountants. Then Sue and the Chief Accountant collate them to form the annual accounts for the Group.

They send each of the subsidiaries forms to fill in, designed to provide the necessary information, with instructions to return them to Head Office by a certain date. Some arrive late and some are incomplete, so Sue spends a lot of time on the telephone, chasing up missing information. She then copies all the relevant figures into one ledger – this was the work she was doing when I visited her. (Some organizations put all the figures into a computer at this stage: *their* accountants are responsible for making sure the computer operators feed in the correct information, and for checking the accounts after they have been processed.) Sue has to

scrutinize the taxation due to be paid by each company, in order to transfer losses from one company to another where they can be set against tax on profits. When the accounts are finished she writes detailed notes explaining the background of the results, including loans, shareholdings, profits and losses. These are for the chairman and directors to use at the Annual General Meeting in case shareholders raise queries. 'I do all this work with the auditors by my side. For about a quarter of every year there is a chartered accountant from an outside firm, sitting at the other desk in my office, checking my work.'

The rest of Sue's time is taken up preparing monthly accounts for the board of directors, with notes on each of the subsidiary companies. She looks at cash flow (the amount of money Associated Fisheries has in the bank, ready to spend) and forecasts when cash will be needed, so that arrangements can be made to borrow if there isn't enough in the bank. She prepares special financial reports every quarter for the Price Commission. She has to study all the new legislation that affects business (there's plenty of it) and, of course, the Chancellor's budgets.

At the annual executives' dinner she is the only woman among 120 men. She has never yet found herself at a disadvantage working in isolation with so many men. 'The people I deal with seem to be glad to talk to a woman for a change. They don't patronize me.'

She believes in keeping her job quite separate from her home life and never meets colleagues on a purely social footing. For Sue accountancy is a pleasant way of earning money so that she can live her 'real' life – evenings, weekends, holidays – in reasonable comfort. That means owning a four-bedroomed house in a quiet street off Clapham Common, and being able to go out to dinner, entertain her friends and travel abroad at least once a year.

Within the next few years she will probably have children, but she has no intention of stopping work. 'Accountancy's an ideal qualification for a woman with a family. Accountants are always in demand – even in a time of economic depression. The basic skills don't change, so it's easy to pick them up again after a break. There is an enormous variety of jobs. You can work for a charity, for solicitors, for property developers, for magazines, for a department store, for the Stock Exchange – you name it. You can use accountancy as a stepping stone to other jobs in business and management. It's always relatively well paid. If you've got small children, you can do what my friend Sue Field has done.'

Sue Field

Sue Field did her articles at Midgeley Snelling, where she first met Sue and Robert Kibble. She, too, married an accountant. Her husband, Tim, works for a merchant bank in the City. When she became pregnant she decided to set up in business on her own, based at her home in Lee, south-east London. She left the firm where she'd been working four months before her baby was due and took over several clients from another accountant called Sally who was leaving England to live abroad. Sue worked on her new clients' accounts throughout the rest of her pregnancy. When she finally went into hospital, Tim used to visit her with armfuls of files and she carried on working in bed.

When I first met Sue, her daughter Charlotte was six months old. Walking up the garden path to her front door, I could see her working with her books and papers spread out on the living room table. When Charlotte demanded her attention, she would some-times sit her on her knee and carry on tapping out the numbers on her calculator. (As she reminded me later, that docile phase of her baby's life ended all too soon!) She hoped to have a second child and planned to work from home indefinitely. 'I can do most of my work here, in my own time. I have to go out once or twice a week to visit clients in their offices and then I pay one of my neighbours to look after Charlotte. When she was smaller I used to take her with me. As soon as she goes to school I'll be able to take on more clients.'

Her overheads are not very costly. She needs a pocket calculator, a typewriter, headed stationery, a telephone, books to keep her up to date with changing tax laws and a fair amount of space to store her files. She finds it helps having a husband in the same line of business. Tim can appreciate the demands of her job and helps her keep in touch with the financial world. 'Even more important,' she says, 'he can help out in a practical way by taking over the care of the baby when she's been screaming all day and I've got behind with my work.'

It would have taken longer to establish a viable practice if she hadn't inherited Sally's clients. Chartered accountants are not allowed to advertise their services; nor are they expected to take their clients with them when they leave a firm (a common practice in advertising). However, Sue doubts that she would have had any difficulty finding work. 'You can approach other chartered accountants and offer to sub-contract work that they are too busy to handle. Your clients pass your name on to other people. The word gets round quite quickly.' Sue found she was much in demand as an accountant for the very reason that she was in an informal setting – a young woman with a child working from home. She does accounts for the feminist magazine *Spare Rib* and for other organizations and individuals who prefer to deal with a woman or who are intimidated by the formal atmosphere of most chartered accountants' offices.

Her biggest problem, it turned out, was that she had under-estimated the amount of time the baby would take up. She committed herself to too many clients too soon and Charlotte was often at her liveliest or most troublesome whenever Sue was hard-pressed to meet deadlines. In retrospect she wishes she had not taken on Sally's clients, but had let the work build up gradually over a year or two. And that, as she points out, would be the normal course of action for most women with young children who decide to start working from home.

Susan White

Craftsman Gardener

If you were to visit Susan at the nurseries where she works you might take the Dover Road through south-east London to Eltham. It's a slow, noisy, irritating journey, so it comes as a great relief to turn into Avery Hill Park.

At the top of Avery Hill stand some fine, imposing red-brick buildings which house the College of Education, and a splendid domed winter garden. These overlook a grand sweep of lawns and playing fields, and the Avery Hill nurseries – where they grow all the plants which are displayed on the property of the Greater London Council.

You would find Susan in the greenhouse, a huge glass building which covers several acres. When you step inside, the atmosphere is hushed, warm and dense. It smells deliciously of earth, moisture and green things growing.

Susan is in charge of the Floral Decoration section. Her plants are not grown for park gardens, but for display in offices, foyers, conference halls and patios. She produces a vast range – from primulas and marigolds to orchids and rubber plants – growing them from seeds or cuttings until they are ready for delivery. They are then driven off in vanloads to the Floral Decoration department at County Hall, which distributes them throughout the GLC area. (So if you happen to see a begonia in a GLC window-box you can assume it started life with Susan.)

Her parents' house had a small garden where her Dad kept a greenhouse, and Susan learnt to grow flowers and vegetables almost before she was taught to read. When she did learn to read, she turned to books about gardening. Yet when she'd taken her three O-levels and it was time to look for a job, no one suggested that she might make a living out of her favourite pastime. Professional gardening was something girls didn't do.

She left school at 16 and went to work as a clerk in the Public Health department of Croydon Borough Council. It wasn't a bad job, but she soon decided there was no future for her in office work. She went to see the local careers officer who pointed her in the right direction. Croydon Borough didn't take girls as apprentice gardeners (this was just before the Sex Discrimination Act came into force), so Susan was advised to try her luck with the GLC. The careers officer didn't sound too optimistic, but she went for a brief interview and got the job straight away.

She began her apprenticeship with 28 boys and one other girl, and was assigned to Horniman Gardens, Forest Hill. The day began at 7.30 with two hours' sweeping to clear litter and debris from lawns, flower beds and paths. It was tough, dirty work and all the gardeners had to do it. Their next job depended on the season. October was leaf-raking time. After a sedentary office job, two weeks' solid leaf-raking almost brought Susan to her knees. Some of the apprentices gave up halfway through the course. But once she had survived that first autumn, she never found the job too strenuous. If there's something she can't handle, the men help her out; and they do the same for each other. There are Health and Safety regulations which instruct them to get help with any job they think they can't handle on their own. Otherwise it's their own responsibility if they injure themselves.

She was taught to plant beds of flowers: first an edging of small flowers, then taller ones, dotted with contrasting colours. She learnt to plant flowers in scroll patterns and – especially for the 1977 Jubilee – to write ER II in red, white and blue flowers. One day a week she went to college to learn the theory: how to identify plants; which ones grow in summer, which in spring; how to look after lawns and playing fields; the composition of fertilizers and composts. She took as many exams as she could and passed with credit. She insists this was not because she was clever, but because she was interested. The City and Guilds exams in Amenity Horticulture (park gardening) were compulsory. In addition she took GLC proficiency exams to assess her progress through the apprenticeship, and Royal Horticultural Society exams which qualified her to work in market gardens or on private estates.

She soon got to know the people who walked through Horniman Gardens each day on their way to work. They stopped for a chat, complimented her on her efforts and told her their own gardening problems. In the summer when the sun shone and Susan was out working in a bikini top and shorts they were all green with envy. 'Ooh, I'd love your job!' she was told several times a day. She reminded them that she had to be out in winter too, sweeping up at 7.30 on icy mornings. Wouldn't they long for their cosy offices then?

She missed them all when she was transferred to Avery Hill in the third year of her apprenticeship. The nurseries aren't open to the public and the plants are not for sale. But she likes everything else about her job there (*and* keeps warm in winter).

The first thing she does each day is what she calls 'spot watering'. The plants are watered automatically via pipes connected to a large machine that regulates the flow, but Susan has to look for dry patches and water them with a watering can. Next she sweeps the floors and picks up dead leaves and petals from the benches. After that she will probably embark on one major job which will take up most of the day. Seeds have to be planted in trays. Cuttings have to be taken from mature plants, dipped in hormone powder to encourage them to put out roots, and placed in trays. When seedlings are big enough they are planted out individually in 'Jiffy Sevens' (little round discs of concentrated compost which swell to the size of a fist when dipped in water). When the plants outgrow their Jiffy Sevens they are transferred to small pots, then to larger ones.

Different plants need different conditions. There's a hot-house and a cold-house. In one section young plants are watered by a misting process – at regular intervals a machine in the corner gives two warning clicks and unless you run for cover you're likely to get drenched.

As Susan showed me round her section of the greenhouse, she occasionally pulled up a leaf cutting from its tray to see if it had put out roots, then stuffed it unceremoniously back into the soil. She's not one for sentimental notions about talking to plants. She can throw them about, she says, and still they flourish; what counts is providing the right growing conditions. Despite her brisk manner, she evidently loves her plants. The rewards of her job are simple and consistent. She puts seeds and cuttings into the earth; they grow in their thousands, produce leaves and flowers, look healthy and beautiful. She watches them bloom and takes pride in them – all her own work!

She gave me tea and biscuits in the manager's office. The foremen stomped in and out in wellington boots, gave friendly greetings and left us alone to talk. Susan normally takes her meals in the 'bothy' – a small room with a cooker, fridge and table where she brews tea, eats sandwiches at lunchtime and cooks herself eggs for breakfast. It's hungry work. She walks literally miles each day, up and down between the benches. There are two bothies, one for the men and one for the women. Of the women, Susan is the only qualified craftsman gardener but there are several others at Avery Hill who do less specialized work. The mealtime segregation isn't compulsory – the women simply like their own company and prefer their bothy which is quieter and more orderly. 'They're great, the people who work in parks,' Susan told me. 'They're more down-to-earth than office types. We always have a good laugh, it's like a big family.' She liked one of her male workmates so much that she decided to marry him. Her fiancé, Chris, works at Horniman Gardens, although he's looking for a foreman's job and may soon move to another park. Susan intends to stay on at Avery Hill. 'Much as I love him, I don't want to work with him. We've already agreed it could be a mistake.'

At one point she thought of trying for a foreman's job her-self. She was sent on a management training course. There were no other women in management jobs in GLC parks at the time, and Susan found that everyone was looking to her as a pioneer. That put her off. 'I'm not sure I'm the sort to blaze a trail. Besides, as a manager you seem to get divorced from the real work. You're looking after people, not plants. That's not what I joined for in the first place. Besides, what would happen if I got a foreman's job and Chris didn't?'

She still lives with her parents and commutes to work by car from their home in Croydon. Her father has worked for most of his life as a painter and sprayer. Her mother is a dressmaker. 'Mum never had any formal qualifications and that's been a disadvantage to her. It made me realize how important it was to do a proper apprenticeship.' Susan grows vegetables on her parents' allotment and tends them in the evenings. When she and Chris get married the first thing they'll look for is a house with a big garden. Out-side working hours, gardening remains their favourite hobby – with a convenient Jack-Sprattish division of labour: 'Chris is the flower man and I'm the vegetable woman.'

When they have children, Susan intends to carry on working. There's a fair supply of part-time and seasonal jobs in GLC parks and her qualifications will stand her in good stead to go back to full-time work later on. She won't go back to office work if she can help it.

'I'm earning more than most of my old school friends now. They all went into office work – clerical jobs in publishing, insurance, travel agencies, things like that. We don't have a lot in common any more. I've changed a lot. They don't really like to get their hands dirty and tend to look down on me. They seem to think I'm a bit like a road sweeper. I couldn't care less what they think, but if they saw me working, they'd soon change their minds.'

When it's your turn to decide

Take a long, careful look at *all* the options open to you. Get as much information as you can about a wide range of jobs and try to get some good, disinterested advice.

If you are at school or in full-time education you have a right to free advice provided through the Careers Service Agency. Look up your nearest office in the telephone directory or enquire at your local school or local education authority. It's important to get advice as early as possible as some forms of training require certain O- or A-level passes, for which you will need to plan ahead.

If you are over 18 and you have left school or college, free occupational guidance is provided through the Employment Services Agency. This is available at 44 centres throughout Britain – you can arrange an interview through your local Employment Exchange or Job Centre.

Maintain a critical attitude to what you are told. Careers teachers or officers may try to channel you into a 'female' job or base their advice purely on current labour needs in your area. If there's a shortage of office staff, they may suggest you become a clerk or typist, which may not be the best thing for you.

Books to Read

The following publications should be available at your school, local Careers Office or public library:

Equal Opportunities, A Careers Guide for Women and Men, by Ruth Miller, Penguin. This is a *must*! It has details of almost every job you can think of and plenty more you've never even dreamt about – more than 100 in all – complete with descriptions of the work involved, qualifications and personal attributes needed, training, prospects, and further sources of information. And it is designed particularly for girls.

Careers A–Z, Daily Telegraph Careers Information Service, Collins. Somewhat male-oriented, nevertheless a useful round-up of jobs and information sources.

Choice of Careers series, published by the Careers and Occupational Information Centre (COIC), Selkirk House, 166 High Holborn, London WC1.

'Working in . . .' series, published by the COIC, for those with no O-levels or only a few.

Information sheets on over 50 graduate careers, published by the Government Central Services Unit.

Decide for Yourself; Your Choice at 13 + (which subjects to choose for CSE or O-level in order to leave your options wide open); *Your Choice at 15 +; Your Choice at 17 +*. All published by the Careers Research and Advisory Centre, Bateman Street, Cambridge.

Careers Encyclopedia, published by Cassell & Co.

Careers Guide, published by the COIC.

Which Degree? published by Haymarket Press.

Directory of First Degree Courses, published annually by the Council for National Academic Awards.

Grants to Students, published annually by the Department of Education and Science.

UCCA Handbook, published by the Universities Central Council on Admissions: a guide to university admission procedure.

Further Education and Training

There are about 600 further education colleges in Britain offering a wide range of courses – both academic and vocational (designed to qualify you for a particular type of work). To find out what is available in your area or field of interest, write to the Department of Education and Science Further Education Information Service,

Room 26, Elizabeth House, 39 York Road, London SE1. They send out useful booklets free of charge.

TOPS : the Government's Training Opportunities Scheme

This scheme is designed to help if you are over 19, have been out of full-time education for at least three years and want to learn a new skill or add to a skill you already have. It works like this:

1) Find a course which suits you. (A TOPS grant will cover you for one year only, so bear this in mind when you select the course.) Then apply for a TOPS grant.

2) Fill in an application form. If you have the right basic qualifications you will be interviewed and tested to assess your aptitude for the course.

3) If you are accepted, you will get a grant which is higher than a student grant (and not means-tested) to support you while you are training. It may include extra allowances – for instance, if you have dependants.

4) You may have to wait for some months before there is a place for you at the college or training centre which provides the necessary course.

5) When you've finished the course, if you reach the required level of competence, you should get help in finding a job.

An immense number of courses are eligible for TOPS grants. Craft courses, which are held at Government Skill Centres and normally last six months, include not only car mechanics, plumbing, carpentry and heavy goods vehicle driving, but catering, TV repair, welding and electrical engineering. There are technical courses ranging from accountancy to design, electronics and estimating : these are usually held at colleges of further education. High-level courses held at polytechnics and universities may also be eligible for TOPS grants if you have the necessary starting qualifications.

There are two ways to approach TOPS: ask at your local Job Centre or Employment Exchange about TOPS courses, read through all the leaflets and pick one which suits you; or find a course you want to do by some other means, then apply for a TOPS grant.

While it is still difficult for women to get accepted as apprentices, TOPS provides a very useful entry into a whole range of traditional 'men's' jobs. The aptitude tests may be exacting, but you are unlikely to encounter sex discrimination.

More information about TOPS at any Job Centre or Employment Exchange.

The Open University

This is open to anyone over 21 and resident in the UK, regardless of qualifications; grants are not available. Teaching is done by a combination of radio and television programmes, weekly seminars and one-week residential summer schools. For details write to the Open University, P.O. Box 48, Milton Keynes MK7 6AB.

Know your legal rights and how to obtain them

(from *The Concise Oxford Dictionary*) **discriminate**, v.t. & i. Be, set up, or observe, a difference between (also intr. with *between*), distinguish *from* another; make a distinction (*~ate against*, distinguish unfavourably, of taxes etc.), observe distinctions carefully.

Every girl can expect to encounter sex discrimination at some stage of her life. It may be subtle, or so taken for granted as to be scarcely noticeable. For example, it may be a tradition among girls at your school to think that subjects like physics and woodwork are not very interesting because they are really intended as boys' subjects. Or it may be that every picture in a careers leaflet distributed by, for example, the Construction Industry Training Board shows only boys and men, as if girls were not welcome in building jobs.

Many forms of discrimination are legal (including the two examples just mentioned). This kind of discrimination will only cease when a majority of people change their attitudes and priorities, which will be a long slow process. But it helps to know that some forms of discrimination *are* against the law. In certain limited but important areas you will find that you have a legal right to be treated no less favourably than a male would be treated in the same circumstances.

Having this legal right does not automatically give you equality. The law isn't magic. *You* have to make the law work for you. And you can do that only if you know what the law says. Below is an outline of your rights under the Sex Discrimination Act and other 'equality laws' which came into force in the mid-1970s. (The Sex Discrimination Act and Equal Pay Act apply to *both* men and women. In this instance, they are described as they apply to women.)

Your right to equal treatment in education

It is illegal to treat you less favourably than a boy would be treated in the same circumstances, by:

1) admitting you to a school or college on different terms; or

2) refusing to admit you; or

3) refusing you access to classes or courses or any other benefits, facilities or services provided by your school or college; or

4) treating you unfavourably in any other way.

The Sex Discrimination Act places a general duty on local education authorities to provide equal education opportunities for both sexes. Unlawful discrimination can be *direct or indirect*:

Direct discrimination is a straightforward matter of treating a girl less favourably than a boy.

Indirect discrimination means imposing certain conditions which can be met by more people of one sex than another. Unlike direct discrimination, it is only against the law if it cannot be shown to be *justifiable*.

Who can be held responsible for breaking the law?

1) The Sex Discrimination Act covers all schools, colleges and other educational establishments maintained by local education authorities (LEAs). The LEA or the school managers or governors can be held responsible depending on the case. Here are two examples:

a) You attend the local co-educational comprehensive school. Every Friday afternoon all the boys do woodwork and all the girls do sewing. No girls are allowed to do woodwork and no boys are allowed to do sewing. In this case the school governors are breaking the law.

b) You go to the local girls' school. Your brother Jack goes to the local boys' school. Your school has poorer science facilities and more science students per teacher than Jack's school, and it does not provide an A-level course in physics, while the boys' school does. In this case the LEA is breaking the law *unless* provisions are made for A-level physics students at the girls' school to make use of the facilities in the boys' school.

2) Independent schools (public and other fee-paying schools) and special schools are also covered by the Act. The proprietors can be held responsible.

3) Universities are covered by the Act. The governing body

95

of the university is responsible for any illegal discrimination.
4) Certain other establishments which have been designated by the Secretary of State for Education are also covered; in each case the governing body can be held responsible.

Exceptions to the law: where discrimination remains legal

1) Single-sex schools and colleges are lawful. They can go on admitting one sex only.

2) Competitive sport: girls can be excluded from participating with boys as competitors in a sport where they would – on average – be at a disadvantage because of physical capacity.

3) Co-educational schools may provide boarding accommodation for one sex only; or accommodation for both sexes which is separate but equal.

4) Single-sex schools becoming co-educational can apply to admit more members of one sex for a limited period.

5) Education provided by charities set up to benefit one sex are exempt.

6) Further education courses in physical training are exempt.

How to get your rights

1) Seek advice on whether your particular case of discrimination is against the law (unless it is so obvious as to leave you in no doubt). Write with a detailed description of your case to the Equal Opportunities Commission (EOC), or the National Union of School Students (NUSS), or an organization such as the National Council for Civil Liberties (NCCL). (Addresses on p.105.)

2) Try to settle the matter informally. Talk to your teachers about it – it may help if you can show them a letter from the EOC which confirms that the discrimination is unlawful. Tell your parents: perhaps they can raise the matter with the Parent Teacher Association. Get support from your fellow students.

3) If nothing changes, you or your parents can bring a formal complaint under the Sex Discrimination Act. If you are under 18 you cannot bring the complaint yourself: one of your parents or your guardian will have to do it for you.

4) If you are at a state school or college, you must start by complaining in writing to the Secretary of State for Education.

5) If nothing is done to end the discrimination within two months of writing, take the complaint to the county court (or the sheriff court in Scotland).

6) At this stage you will almost certainly need help to proceed with your case. Ask the EOC if they will help you, either by conducting the case themselves or by helping with your legal fees. If that fails, write to the NUSS or the NCCL; or seek advice from a solicitor. You may get legal advice free or partly free under the 'green form' procedure ('pink form' procedure in Scotland). You will find further information and advice in the publications listed on p.105.

Remember, victimization is illegal

The Sex Discrimination Act says it is illegal to treat anyone less favourably just because they have taken action under either the Sex Discrimination Act or the Equal Pay Act. 'Taking action' may include bringing a formal complaint, helping someone else to do so, accusing someone of breaking the laws, or taking any other action in connection with either law.

Your right to equal treatment in training and employment

The Sex Discrimination Act says it is illegal, in the fields of training and employment, to treat a woman less favourably than a man would be treated in the same circumstances, or to treat a married woman less favourably than a single woman. The Act covers temporary and permanent employees, apprentices and trainees, partners in firms with six or more partners; and self-employed workers who are contracted to do a particular job (such as 'lump' building workers).

It applies to training; recruitment; considering applicants for jobs; hiring; additional benefits, such as extra time off or help with housing; promotion or transfer to another job; putting workers on short time; redundancy and dismissal; and any other conditions of employment or money payments which are *not* included in your contract.

The Equal Pay Act covers all conditions of employment and training which *are* covered by your contract. See p.100.

Unlawful discrimination may be *direct* or *indirect*, as with education. Here are some examples to help you distinguish between the two:

1) You apply for an apprenticeship in welding. You are refused. Only boys are taken on and their qualifications are no better than yours. This is *direct* discrimination.

2) A company recruits trainees from local schools. It insists that *all* applicants should have O-level physics and chemistry. The local schools are not co-educational. Both subjects are available at the girls' schools but very few girls take them as it is traditional for them to opt for biology. This is *indirect* discrimination. If the employer cannot show that it is justiliable (ie that trainees really do need a knowledge of physics and chemistry to do the job) he is breaking the law.

3) You apply for a job. You have all the right qualifications but you are not given an interview. Only men are interviewed and a man is hired. No woman has held the job before. This is *direct* discrimination.

4) You work as a tracer in an engineering company and you apply for promotion to become a draughtswoman. You are told that only those who have served an apprenticeship on the shop floor are eligible for promotion. Neither you nor any other woman has ever served an apprenticeship with the company. This is *indirect* discrimination. Unless the employer can show that such an apprenticeship is an essential qualification for a draughtswoman, he is breaking the law.

Exceptions to the law: where discrimination remains legal

1) Treating a single woman less favourably than a married woman.

2) Conditions relating to pregnancy and childbirth.

3) Conditions relating to retirement and pensions.

4) Employment in private households.

5) Where an employer has fewer than six employees.

6) Jobs in the armed forces.

7) Employment in active mines.

8) Working for a church which has a sex bar because of its religious doctrine or in order to avoid 'offending the religious susceptibilities of a significant number of its followers'.

9) Only women are allowed to be midwives, except in certain colleges and hospitals approved by the Department of Health.

10) Where sex is a *Genuine Occupational Qualification* (GOQ) for the job. This exempts a whole range of jobs, including modelling and acting; jobs involving physical contact with one sex (although this cannot be used against medical staff); lavatory and changing room attendants; jobs on ships, lighthouses and remote work sites where it is unreasonable to expect the employer to provide separate accommodation for women; jobs in some single-sex institutions such as hospitals

and children's homes; certain jobs where a welfare, educational or similar service can 'most effectively' be provided by a man; work which has to be done by a man because of the protective laws which impose restrictions on women factory workers; work which is likely to involve travel to countries 'whose laws are such that the duties could not be performed effectively by a woman'; and where a job is one of two to be held by a married couple.

Organizations covered by the Sex Discrimination Act

As well as covering employers in the UK with six or more employees, the Act applies to:

1) *Training Bodies* such as industrial training boards and the Training Services Agency.

2) *Employment Agencies* It is unlawful for an employment agency to discriminate against you by the terms it offers; by the way it provides any of its services; or by deliberately omitting to provide services.

3) *Licensing Bodies* which authorize people to do particular types of work, such as the Law Society which issues certificates of practice to solicitors; and the police, who license taxi drivers.

4) *The Government* must not discriminate against women in making public appointments – *eg* to bodies such as the BBC or the boards of nationalized industries.

5) *Trade Unions, Employers' Organizations and Professional Associations* must not discriminate in admission to membership or treatment of members.

Positive discrimination in favour of women is allowed in some circumstances

Training bodies and employers can take positive steps to encourage women to apply for jobs or training courses, or to give women special training, where they have formerly been at a disadvantage.

Trade unions and professional associations may discriminate in favour of women by organizing special training for them; encouraging them to apply for jobs within the organization; holding recruiting drives for women only; and reserving a quota of seats for women on elected committees.

Job advertisements

It is illegal to advertise a job in a way which indicates that the employer intends to discriminate unlawfully. For instance an advertisement which refers to the applicant as 'he' without saying that the job is also open to women is probably illegal. This does not apply to ads for jobs abroad.

Your right to equal pay

The Equal Pay Act says you should be paid the same as a man if:
1) you are doing the same or broadly similar work; or
2) your work has been given the same value as his by a job evaluation scheme.

In addition to equal pay, the Act covers any other terms and conditions which are contained in your contract. These might include holidays, shiftwork, premiums, bonuses, luncheon vouchers.

How to get your rights

1) If you belong to a trade union, you may find that collective bargaining provides the best way of getting your rights. So tell your union representative that you think your employer is breaking the law. In any event, you should be in a stronger position to claim your legal rights if you belong to a union. If the union cannot get you a fair deal by means of negotiation, it should be able to give you advice and help you make a formal complaint under the terms laid down by the law.

2) Complaints about unlawful discrimination in training and employment, and claims for equal pay can be made to an *industrial tribunal*. File your complaint within three months of the date on which the discrimination occurred. Get the complaint form (IT 1) from your nearest Employment Exchange or Job Centre.

3) Make sure you get good advice. If your trade union cannot provide this, try the Advisory, Conciliation and Arbitration Service (ACAS), which answers queries about the provisions of the two laws; write to the regional manager at your nearest regional office. Alternatively, write to the Equal Opportunites Commission or the NCCL. (Addresses on p.105.) You may be able to get advice from a solicitor and help in preparing your case, either free or partly free under the 'green form' procedure (in Scotland, the 'pink form' procedure).

4) You will find further information and advice in the publications listed on p.105.

5) Remember, victimization is illegal. If you think you have

been victimized for taking action under the Sex Discrimination or Equal Pay Act, you can complain formally to an industrial tribunal.

Maternity rights

If you become pregnant while you are working, you have the following legal rights:

Protection against unfair dismissal
If you have been working for your employer for at least six months and your employer sacks you when you become pregnant, this is *unfair dismissal* and you can claim damages and/or reinstatement at an industrial tribunal, *unless* you were sacked because:
> a) your pregnancy makes you incapable of 'adequately doing the work' (*eg* your job involves constant lifting of heavy objects); or
> b) it is illegal and unusually dangerous for your job to be done by a pregnant woman (*eg* you are a radiologist).

Even if you were sacked for one of these reasons, it is still unfair dismissal unless your employer first offered you an alternative job – if there was one available – on terms and conditions 'not substantially less favourable' than your previous job. If no alternative job is available, then the dismissal is *fair*: you cannot claim damages, but you may be able to claim reinstatement up to 29 weeks after your baby is born if you satisfy the conditions below.

Reinstatement after 29 weeks
You have a right to be reinstated in your job up to 29 weeks after your baby's birth, on the following conditions:
> 1) You have been working for the same employer for at least two years at the beginning of the 11th week before the baby is due.
> 2) You carried on working up until the beginning of that 11th week. (You need not satisfy this condition if you were 'fairly' dismissed before the 11th week.)
> 3) You informed your employer (in writing if he requested it) that you intended to exercise your right to return to work. You must do this twice: at least three weeks before you leave work (or as soon as is reasonably practicable if you are 'caught short'); and at least one week before you intend going back to work.

4) If your employer asks, you must produce a certificate signed by your doctor or midwife giving the estimated date of the baby's birth.

You may not get the very same job back. You have a right to return to the same job you were doing before *as it is described in your contract*. If the description is fairly general, it could give your employer some scope – so check the wording of your contract. For instance, if your contract simply describes you as a *technician* employed by Smith, Brown & Co., you may find you have to return to a job in another department.

Maternity pay

You have a right to six weeks' maternity pay, provided you satisfy all the conditions listed above for reinstatement – with one exception: you do not have to return to work after the birth. Just tell your employer at least three weeks before the baby is due (or as soon as practicable) that you intend to stop work because you're having a baby. Maternity pay will be 90 per cent of your basic weekly pay.

How to get your rights

If your employer refuses to give you your legal entitlements, you can bring a claim to an industrial tribunal. (See p.100.)

These rights are only the legal minimum. Many employees have negotiated more generous provisions for maternity leave and pay. If this isn't the case at your workplace, why not take up the matter with your trade union?

National Insurance maternity benefits

If you have been paying full National Insurance contributions for at least two years before your baby is due, you can claim the State maternity allowance and maternity grant. The latter is a lump sum of £25; the former is a weekly payment equivalent to unemployment benefit: it goes up each year.

Being a working mother

So you've established yourself in a job you enjoy, you've taken your maternity leave, you've had your baby, you've claimed your right to maternity pay and reinstatement, and now you're back at work. How, for the next 16 years are you going to manage to carry on working and give your children the care they deserve? In this wonderful new age of sex equality it is *here* that the system breaks down!

Two of the women in this book, Sue Field and Anna Cunning-ham, have found their own solutions to the problem by working from home. It suits them, but it wouldn't suit everyone. Engineers and airline pilots can't readily start one-woman businesses and, besides, many women feel isolated at home, looking after children on their own. Liane Bracken has an unusually flexible working arrangement. Not many women could find suitable, satisfying jobs which allowed them a similar freedom. Jocelyn Burnell has a part-time job. Some women could not afford to live on part-time pay, and part-time jobs are quite scarce.

What working women need more than anything else is good, inexpensive, comprehensive child care, both for under-fives and for school-age children during holidays, half-terms and those awkward hours between the end of school and the end of the working day in most factories and offices.

Given that child care provision is hopelessly inadequate, what alternatives are open to you?

Local authority day nurseries

These are the only State-run nurseries which cater for children of women who have full-time jobs. They are run by the social services departments of local authorities and they are usually open between 8 a.m. and 6 p.m., including school holidays. They take children from six weeks old to school age. They are not free, but the amount you pay depends on your income.

Standards vary and places are restricted. Day nurseries have to give priority to children from 'deprived backgrounds', which means children of single parents who have to go out to work; children whose mothers are ill; and children who live in poor housing conditions. They also have to give priority to children of teachers if there is a shortage of teachers in the area. You will find it almost impossible to get a place for your child unless you fit into one of these categories – but it's worth enquiring. Contact the social services department of your local authority: you'll find the address in the telephone directory under the name of the authority. It helps if you have a recommendation from a doctor, health visitor or social worker.

Childminders

Childminders are people who look after children by taking them into their homes as a means of income. They still supply the most common form of child care used by working mothers. Prices and standards vary. Childminders are legally obliged to register with the local authority so that their homes can be checked for safety against fire risk and overcrowding. However, a lot of child-minders don't register. You can get a list of registered childminders with vacancies from your local authority social services department.

After-school and holiday care for schoolchildren

A few local authorities provide play centres for children during these times; places are limited. Enquire at your local authority social services department. If there isn't one in your area, perhaps you could get together with other parents and ask the council to set one up.

Nurseries at the workplace

There are very few of these, but increasing numbers of women are asking their employers to provide child care facilities. Why not start negotiations through your trade union? There may be other employers nearby who could be persuaded to share the costs. You will have to be very determined and well organized. At the time of writing, the National Union of Journalists was preparing a step-by-step guide to setting up a nursery; write for a copy to Acorn House, Gray's Inn Road, London WC1.

Any other ideas?

If you are reasonably well-off you may be able to afford a mother's help; or pay a non-employed neighbour to look after your children for an hour or two after school. If that doesn't help, perhaps you could persuade your employer to let you work part-time, sharing your job with another similarly qualified part-time worker: job-sharing is quite common in Scandanavia these days. Another possibility is to share accommodation with a friend who has children but does not work (if you can make mutually acceptable arrangements which do not exploit her!). If you are married, perhaps you and your husband could 'swap roles' for a year or two: he staying at home to look after the child while you go out to work and support the family. There are quite a few families who do this now – and why not? Some men are more suited to domestic life and parental duties than some women – it depends on your respective personalities and needs. But these are all makeshift suggestions. A far more satisfactory solution would be the adequate provision of nurseries and play centres for all children.

Further information and advice

The Equal Opportunities Commission, Overseas House, Quay Street, Manchester M3 3HN.

ACAS (Advisory, Conciliation and Arbitration Service): head office Cleland House, Page Street, London SW1. It also has offices in Newcastle, Leeds, Manchester, Birmingham, Bristol, Glasgow and Cardiff. Addresses in local telephone directories or from head office.

National Council for Civil Liberties, 186 Kings Cross Road, London WC1.

TUC (Trades Union Congress), 23–28 Great Russell Street, London WC1.

National Union of School Students, National Union of Students, 3 Endsleigh Street, London WC1.

Women's Rights: A Practical Guide by Anna Coote and Tess Gill, Penguin (£1.25). A comprehensive guide to women's legal rights, with detailed advice on how to pursue claims through industrial tribunals and the courts.

Maternity Rights for Working Women, by Jean Coussins, NCCL (30p). A complete guide to claiming maternity benefits, plus a critique of the legal provisions.

The Unequal Breadwinner by Ruth Lister NCCL (30p); summary of the rights of 'role swap' couples.

The Women's Directory by Carolyn Faulder, Christine Jackson and Mary Lewis, Virago (£1.95). A directory and handbook with names, addresses and telephone numbers of the organizations, groups and resources of women's activities in the UK, plus discussion of a wide range of relevant issues.

More information about the jobs in this book

The individual experiences of the women in this book may not be typical. If you want to follow in their footsteps, please don't imagine you will encounter the difficulties they did, or that you will necessarily get the same lucky breaks. On the whole, you are likely to find it easier to get into these jobs – as long as you have the right attributes – since much of the pioneering work for women has been done.

In many cases, training methods have changed and become more structured. Details are set out on the following pages.

Production Engineer

The best source of information for all jobs in engineering is The Engineering Careers Information Service which is attached to the Engineering Industry Training Board (EITB), 54 Clarendon Road, Watford, WD1 1LB.

Jobs in engineering   There is a very wide range of engineering work. The industry makes almost everything you can think of which uses metal or a combination of metal and plastics – from cars, aeroplanes and power stations to electronic equipment, record players, film cameras, quarrying and agricultural machinery, TV sets, kitchen appliances, telephone equipment, ships, roads and bridges.

As an engineer you may end up working in a factory, a hospital, an airport, a laboratory, television studio, local authority or small design consultancy. You may work with heavy machinery or with minute components, with chemicals, computers, or pen and paper. Some engineering jobs need high academic ability and an aptitude for research; some require creative flair and design skills; others need organizational skills. Some jobs will suit you if you are good at taking a logical, practical approach to solving problems; others enable you to develop manual skills.

There are three main channels of entry into engineering, designed to suit different aptitudes. You can aim to be a professional engineer; a technician engineer or technician; or a craft engineer. Barbara Stephens trained as a technician engineer.

Technician Engineers and Technicians

They provide the link in the production process between the professional engineer and the craft engineer. They work closely together, though their training tends to be different and the technician engineer usually has a wider range of responsibilities. The EITB explains: 'In a design department, for example, a Technician Engineer might be given the task of designing a fuel pump or a car engine. The Technician would produce detailed drawings for the pump's individual components. In a test department, a Technician Engineer will co-ordinate and supervise a test programme on an aircraft undercarriage system. The Technician will help him (sic) by setting up test equipment and conducting the tests.'

You may work at a drawing board designing, or assisting to design, components and products. Or you may work as a production engineer, like Barbara. Technician engineers and technicians are also employed in quality control, sales, maintenance, repair and servicing. If you find writing easy, you might want to become a technical writer, producing technical booklets, instruction manuals, sales brochures, etc.

Training You will normally need at least four O-levels, including maths and science. Training schemes vary. As a rule, you apply for an apprenticeship with a company and then undergo between two and four years' training, partly in college and partly in the company's own training centre and factory.

There's a variety of TOPS courses (p.92) for training technicians. The EITB provides a number of scholarships for girls who want to train as technicians – in an attempt to attract more females into engineering. More information on this from the EITB (address on p.106).

Prospects   Excellent. Technician engineers and technicians are much in demand in all branches of industry. There are opportunities to progress to administrative and managerial jobs as well as to senior technical posts.

Flexibility   If you have a break from work while your children are young it shouldn't be too difficult (especially for technicians) to return, provided you keep up to date with developments in your field. Part-time jobs are rare.

Pay   Medium.

Professional Engineer

This is the top level of engineering, requiring the highest academic ability and providing the most far-reaching opportunities. As a professional engineer you may work in research and development, devising new processes and products; you may be a designer or a production engineer; or you may go into marketing. There is some overlap between the work of professional engineers and technician engineers.

Each branch of professional engineering has its own Institute which can provide you with more information. Names and addresses are in the *Annual Careers Guide*, published by HMSO, which should be available at your local Careers Office or public library, if you can't find it at your school.

Training   To qualify you need a degree in engineering from a university or polytechnic, plus practical experience. Sandwich courses which combine theoretical education with practical training are particularly suitable. Some companies sponsor students for degree courses; others take on graduates for further training. Graduate trainees usually spend at least a year going round the factory studying the various methods and practices of each department.

Prospects   Excellent. There is a severe shortage of professional engineers in British industry. There should be opportunities for advancement to the most senior technical and managerial jobs – although promotion is likely to be more difficult for women than for men.

Flexibility   As for technician engineer.

Pay   Medium to good.

Craft Engineer

This is the practical end of the industry. As a craft engineer you are highly skilled in one particular type of work, with enough theoretical knowledge to understand the principles behind it. It may be your job to operate a sophisticated piece of machinery to very exact specifications, 'perhaps,' as the EITB says, 'machining the component parts of an electric motor or generator, knowing that each part must fit perfectly and that your slightest error could make it useless'. You may work in a factory as a skilled fitter, welder, sheet metal worker, toolmaker or maintenance engineer. Or you may work on a building site, in a small workshop or in private homes as an electrician, a mechanic or a plumber. (See p.118 and p.124 for more about plumbing and mechanics.)

Training   You need average ability in mathematics, science and technical/practical subjects, preferably with CSE or O-level passes, although employers often give applicants an aptitude test. The usual training is a three to four year apprenticeship with an engineering firm. However, it is still hard for girls to get accepted as craft apprentices. The TOPS courses (p.92) provide a useful way in by enabling you to get a job as a trainee, so that you can complete your qualifications later by taking day-release or evening classes at college.

Prospects   Once you've had some training, you should be able to get a job without much difficulty, although there are more opportunities in some parts of the country than in others. There are few girls at this level of engineering and very few in factories. You may encounter prejudice from prospective employers and workmates. It will probably be more difficult for you to get promotion to the post of chargehand or supervisor than for a man with the same qualifications. However, attitudes are gradually becoming more enlightened.

Flexibility   Once qualified, a break in your employment should not present problems. Some crafts give you the opportunity to regulate your own hours – for instance, an electrician might become self-employed like Anna Cunningham (pp. 30–35).

Pay   Poor while training; then medium, occasionally good.

Lorry Driver

Information from the Road Transport Industry Training Board, Capitol House, Empire Way, Wembley, Middlesex.

The work   As Lesley Smith says, the lorry driver's job may involve not only driving but roping and sheeting, and loading and unloading goods – unless you are driving container vehicles only. The job carries a lot of responsibility. You must be able to drive safely and look after your vehicle and its load (although you don't need detailed mechanical knowledge). You need to be physically fit, very patient, unflappable, independent, to enjoy travelling and being alone for long periods.

There are three common categories of heavy goods vehicle (HGV): Class I, the largest-sized; Class II, medium-sized; and Class III, smaller trucks and vans.

Training   No academic qualifications are needed. If you are 21 or over you can take the Class I HGV test, but not before that. Enquire at your local office of the Training Services Agency or Job Centre for details about training. TOPS grants are available (see p. 92).

For school leavers, the Road Transport Industry Training Board has launched the 'Young Driver Scheme', to encourage employers in road haulage firms to take on 16-year-olds as trainee HGV drivers. You spend the first year attending college, and doing general duties for the employer or accompanying qualified drivers. Meanwhile you are trained to take the ordinary Class A driving test when you are 17; this qualifies you to drive cars and light vans. At 18 you are trained to drive Class III HGVs; at 19 you may progress, if your employer wishes, to drive Class II HGVs and finally at 21 you take the Class I test. If you don't spend the first year at college you will follow a day-release further education programme to learn about the road freight transport industry, basic mechanics, laws and regulations affecting HGV drivers, route planning, etc. Get details of employers operating the Young Driver Scheme from your careers officer.

Prospects   Fair. HGV drivers with some experience should have no difficulty finding work. Driving skills are versatile: once you've acquired them you can use them to help you get other driving jobs (see below).

Flexibility   A break in your employment to have children should cause no problems. However, long-distance driving will be virtually impossible if you have small children and no one to look after them while you are away.

Pay   Medium.

Other driving jobs
Driving Instructor   You need four years' driving record without

any endorsements on your licence. Theoretically you can take the instructor's test when you are 21 although licences are rarely granted to anyone under 25. Many instructors work on their own, after purchasing cars with dual controls. This is more lucrative though less secure than working for one of the big driving schools. Hours are irregular and can be long as learners often need lessons after working hours and at weekends. It is essential to have someone at home to deal with telephone bookings. To be an instructor you need to be a good teacher, not just a good driver. You must be patient, calm and able to get on with all types of people and put them at their ease. You will have to pass a stringent written and practical examination set by the Department of the Environment.

Further information from the Department of the Environment (Register of Driving Instructors), Lambeth Bridge House, London SE1.

Bus Driver Enquire at your local bus company.

Taxi Driver Ask your nearest taxi firms or write to the Taxi Drivers' Association, 9 Woodville Road, London W9.

Ambulance Driver Enquire at your local Area Health Authority.

Your careers officer should also be able to supply information about these jobs.

Solicitor

For information on entry to the profession:

The Law Society, Law Society's Hall, 113 Chancery Lane, London WC2A 1PL.

If you want to work in Scotland or Northern Ireland, where the law is substantially different, address your enquiries to:

The Law Society of Scotland, 26–27 Drumsheugh Gardens, Edinburgh EH3 7YB; or

The Incorporated Law Society of Northern Ireland, Legal Aid Department, Law Courts Buildings, Belfast.

The work There is a very wide range of work available to qualified solicitors. Most solicitors work (like Roberta McDonald) in private firms or partnerships, some of which specialize in particular areas of the law such as criminal law, matrimonal and family law, company law, taxation, conveyancing, international law, welfare, housing and consumer law, or employment law. Some solicitors work as legal officers or advisers in trade unions and a few voluntary organizations; they are also employed in the Civil Service, the EEC bureaucracy, commercial companies and the small but growing number of neighbourhood law centres.

To be a solicitor you need the capacity to absorb facts quickly and a good memory, a logical mind, an ability to express yourself clearly (at least in legal language), plenty of patience and – obvious, but important – a keen interest in the law and legal procedures.

Training   The training structure is changing so make sure you get up-to-date information from the Law Society. It is best to start by taking a degree, then:

a) if you take a law degree, you follow it with a 36-week full-time course at a college of law or polytechnic, culminating in the Final Examination, and a further two years as an articled clerk (*ie* doing practical training in a solicitor's office). Your law degree must be approved by the Law Society, so check this before you embark on your university course.

b) If your degree is not an approved law degree (and it can be in any subject) you must take a one-year full-time course at a college of law or polytechnic, leading to the Common Professional Exam; then do the Final Examination and two years' articles (as do graduates with approved law degrees).

Choose carefully where you do your articles. If, for instance, you're most interested in family law, it wouldn't be very useful to do articles in a firm which specializes in heavy commercial work. Some firms give their articled clerks better training than others; some use them as office drudges, or restrict their legal work to a very narrow field.

Prospects   Good. As a competent solicitor you are unlikely ever to have difficulty finding work. With experience, you can advance to highly paid senior positions. You can set up a law firm of your own if you can accumulate the capital and some contacts, and are prepared to work very hard.

Flexibility   Part-time work is possible, although your time will need to be fairly flexible, since appointments at courts and tribunals often determine your working hours. A break in your employment should present no problems as long as you keep up with legal developments.

Pay   Medium to high, if most of the work you do is legally aided (see p.26). If you do commercial work, conveyancing or other cases for fee-paying clients, remuneration can be very high. Articled clerks are usually paid a pittance.

Related fields

Legal Executive

Information from The Institute of Legal Executives, Ilex House, Barrhill Road, London SW2 4RW.

The work   As a legal executive you work as a solicitor's assistant, doing the essential groundwork for cases, *eg* looking up references, preparing documents, interviewing witnesses, conferring with clients on points of detail. The amount of responsibility and the variety of work depend upon the solicitors you work for as well as on your own level of competence. You may do everything a solicitor does, short of appearing in open court. Many legal secretaries become legal executives.

Training   You need four academic O-levels, and the usual way to start is by getting a job as a clerk in a solicitor's office. After six months' practical experience as a clerk or legal secretary you can enrol as a student with the Institute of Legal Executives (address above). Training is on-the-job with day-release or evening classes or an approved correspondence course. There are two stages of qualification: the Associate exam, which is the intermediate stage, is usually taken during the first three years; and the Fellowship exam, taken after another five years, allows you to call yourself a legal executive and put the letters F. Inst. L. Ex. after your name.

Prospects   Fair. Promotion from assistant to senior legal executive can be slow, it depends on the firm. No direct promotion to solicitor.

Flexibility   Some opportunity for part-time work.

Pay   Low to high, depending on your seniority and the type of organization for which you work.

Barrister

Information from the Council of Legal Education, 4 Gray's Inn Place, London WC1R 5DX. Training and organization is different in Scotland, so apply to the Faculty of Advocates, Parliament House, Edinburgh EH1 1RF.

The work   As a barrister you plead the case for the prosecution or the defence in court, and give advice to solicitors on legal matters. As well as a passionate interest in the law you need plenty of self-confidence, the ability to think fast on your feet and an aptitude for logical argument. You must be articulate and have the capacity to inspire confidence. If you have some acting ability, that helps too.

Some barristers do less court work and concentrate more on providing legal opinions. Some work for the Civil Service as advisers.

Training   You must have a degree. If it's an approved law degree you follow it with a course which lasts about one academic year at the Inns of Court School of Law or the College of Law, leading to an examination. After that you must do a year's pupillage in Chambers (*ie* practical experience in barristers' offices) which costs about £100. If your degree is not an approved law degree, you must start off with an extra year's study and take a Diploma in Law before following the same training as a law graduate.

Prospects   The Bar operates like a rather exclusive club. Barristers have to be attached to a set of Chambers and the number of tenancies is very limited. You need good contacts or a lot of determination and luck. Practising barristers are self-employed and depend on work from solicitors, which is farmed out to them by barristers' clerks (who operate rather like actors' agents). If you are good at the work the prospects are excellent once you're established. At the top of the profession are QCs (Queen's Counsels) who command enormous fees, and judges.

Flexibility   There is little or no opportunity for part-time work and if you have a break in your career it could be difficult getting started again. The chances may be better for legal advisers employed by the Civil Service.

Pay   Poor to medium while getting established, then medium to very high.

Furniture Restorer

If you want to do the same sort of work as Anna Cunningham there are two ways to approach it.

1) Direct entry: try to get an apprenticeship with an experienced furniture/antique restorer, or find a course in furniture restoration at a college (and apply for a grant) then get work as an assistant to an experienced restorer.

2) Start with a training in carpentry, either by getting an apprenticeship with a building firm or craftsman's workshop, or by going on a TOPS course (p.92) at a Government Skill Centre. Then move on to furniture restoration.

Flexibility   Impossible to generalize.

Prospects and Pay are generally good once you have the basic training and some experience. Furniture restoration is a fairly narrow specialization. If you want to work with wood or with furniture generally, there is a good variety of other jobs you can think about.

Related fields

Carpentry   Trained carpenters are employed by local authorities and building firms; they lay floorboards, hang doors, fit windows, erect roof timbers and staircases, and make built-in furniture. Sometimes they work on construction sites; at other times they work in homes which are being converted or redecorated. With enough experience as a carpenter you may be able to set up in business on your own, doing repairs in private houses and building cupboards or other units to customers' specifications. The Construction Industry Training Board, Glen House, Stag Place, London SW1, has information about apprenticeships and other training schemes in carpentry and industrial woodwork. The CITB also has offices in Glasgow, Harrogate, Liverpool, Rugby, Bath, Luton: apply to your nearest office; addresses are obtainable from Careers Offices or Job Centres.

Cabinet-making   Cabinet-makers produce high quality wooden furniture using traditional techniques. Normal entry is by apprenticeship, although it may be possible to use TOPS (p.92). Details of training schemes from the British Furniture Trade Joint Industrial Council, 17 Berners Street, London W1.

Furniture Design   To do this you will need more design ability than manual skill and you will have to take a course at college leading to a diploma or degree. Further details from the Chartered Society of Industrial Artists and Designers, 12 Carlton House Terrace, London SW1.

Art Restoration   This is even more highly skilled and specialized than furniture/antique restoration and it may involve restoring paintings and priceless museum pieces. For advice on courses, write to the Museums' Association, 87 Charlotte Street, London W1P 2BX.

Forestry

The best source of information about jobs in forestry is The Forestry Commission Headquarters, 231 Corstorphine Road, Edinburgh EH12 7AT. Half of the productive forests in Britain are publicly owned and managed by the Forestry Commission.

Useful addresses for obtaining information about jobs in the private sector:

Home Timber Merchants Association of England and Wales, Blackburn House, 1 Warwick Street, Leamington Spa, Warwickshire.

Home Timber Merchants Association of Scotland, 16 Gordon Street, Glasgow G3 QE.

Economic Forestry Group, Forestry House, Great Milton, Oxford OX9 7PG.

Scottish Woodland Owners Association Ltd, 6 Chester Street, Edinburgh EH3 7RD.

Timber Growers Organization Ltd, National Agricultural Centre, Kenilworth, Warwicks CV8 2LG.

Tilhill Forestry Group, Greenhills, Tilford, Farnham, Surrey; and Old Sauchie, Sauchieburn, Stirling, Scotland.

There are three main grades of work in forestry: the forestry officer, the forester and the forestry worker. (Fiona Fenton is a forester.)

Forester

Foresters are technical forest managers. Experienced foresters are also employed in specialist duties such as work study, conservation, research and training.

To be a forester you will need to be interested in science, conservancy and wildlife; to be able to manage alone in remote areas and to deal with members of the general public. Management skills and ease in communicating with gangs of forest workers in your charge are also necessary, as are willingness to travel and a liking for outdoor life in all weathers. The age limit for becoming a forester with the Forestry Commission is 35. You need a driving licence, too.

Training   Most foresters start out as forest workers (but see alternative below) and after two years' practical experience take a three-year sandwich course (one year's practical between two years' theoretical training) at the Cumbria College of Agriculture and Forestry. Candidates for the course, which leads to an Ordinary National Diploma (OND) in forestry, need at least four O-levels or four Grade I CSE passes, two of which should be science subjects and one of which should test the command of English (eg history, geography, religious knowledge). Further information about the course from the Principal of Cumbria College of Agriculture and

Forestry, Newton Rigg, Penrith, Cumbria. If you get an offer of a place before you've had any practical experience, the Forestry Commission may consider you for a job as a forest worker. Apply to the Chief Education and Training Officer at the Forestry Commission (address on p.115).

As an alternative, you can qualify for a forester's job by taking a degree in forestry. These courses are provided at Aberdeen, Edinburgh, Oxford and Bangor (Wales) universities. A degree in forestry also enables you to apply for a job as a forest officer (see immediately below).

Prospects Jobs with the Forestry Commission are not easy to come by. If you have a degree you can seek promotion to forest officer (assuming you can get a job in the first place).

Flexibility The Commission expects foresters to move jobs approximately once every five years – although this is not now as strict a condition as it used to be.

Pay Medium.

Forest Officer

The majority of District forest officers plan and control the planting and conservation work and the preparation of forest produce in groupings of forests known as Districts. They have responsibility for private woodlands in their District and may also be involved in the acquisition of land for forestry. Many District officers are employed in more specialized work such as recreation, training, forest research and development. The job requires organizational skill, the ability to deal with people and to take responsibility. Age limit for entry to the job is 31. You need a driving licence.

Training You need a university degree in forestry, or a degree in a closely allied subject with a postgraduate qualification in a forestry subject.

Prospects A reasonable chance of promotion to more senior posts within the Forestry Commission.

Flexibility As above, though you may be expected to move less frequently.

Pay Medium to good.

Forest Worker

Forest workers do all the manual work and machine operation in the forest. This includes fencing, planting, draining, weeding, pruning, timber harvesting and nursery work. A high degree of skill with forest tools and machines is necessary.

Training   You should have a chance to train and study for City and Guilds exams which qualify you as a 'Craftsman'. Apply *not* to the Forestry Commission Headquarters but to the Conservancy, District or Forest Office; addresses can be found in local telephone directories.

Prospects   At the time of writing there were virtually no female forest workers employed by the Forestry Commission. But if you think you are physically capable of doing the job there is no reason why you shouldn't apply.

Flexibility   Impossible to predict.

Pay   Poor.

Related fields

The Forestry Commission also employs a range of scientific and technical staff as well as cartographic (map drawing) staff; engineering staff, land agents and clerks of work. Details of all these jobs from the Forestry Commission Headquarters (address on p.115).

Useful addresses for information on jobs connected with conservation and wildlife outside the Forestry Commission can be obtained from:

Nature Conservancy, 19 Belgrave Square, London SW1.

Council for Nature, Zoological Gardens, Regent's Park, London NW1.

Royal Society for the Protection of Birds, The Lodge, Sandy, Bedfordshire.

Society for the Promotion of Nature Reserves, The Manor House, Alford, Lincs.

Local authorities (addresses in telephone directory).

Countryside Commission, 1 Cambridge Gate, Regent's Park, London NW1 4JY.

Plumber

Information from the Construction Industry Training Board, Glen House, Stag Place, London SW1. The CITB also has offices in Glasgow, Harrogate, Liverpool, Rugby, Bath and Luton: addresses from the telephone directory, your local Careers Office or Job Centre. Information also from:

The Joint Industry Board for Plumbing and Mechanical Engineering Services in England and Wales, Brook House, Brook Street, St Neots, Huntingdon, Cambridgeshire.

The Scottish Joint Industry Board for the Plumbing Industry, 2 Walker Street, Edinburgh EH3 7LB.

The work Plumbers work not only in private homes, but also on building sites, where they are an essential part of any construction team, helping to build everything from individual houses to schools, hospitals and power stations. Plumbers install pipes, lay drains, put the metal waterproofing into roofs, build guttering, fit central heating systems, boilers, tanks and cisterns as well as toilets, sinks, baths and showers. They are employed by local authorities as well as by private firms. To be a plumber you need to be physically fit and reasonably (though not unusually) strong; to enjoy working with your hands in fairly rough conditions and not mind getting dirty.

Training There are no essential requirements but you will need average ability in maths and science. CSE or O-level passes in these subjects are an advantage. When you leave school, try to find an apprenticeship with a firm of plumbers or builders which operates the CITB scheme. This will give you six months off-the-job study followed by two years on-the-job experience, with day-release training, leading to the CITB Craft Certificate. Otherwise you will have to serve a three-year apprenticeship and study the theory at evening classes or (if your employer allows) you can study at a day-release course. TOPS (p.92) provides a useful start, especially as some employers are reluctant to take on girl apprentices.

Prospects Fairly good. Plumbers are always in demand, although the number of jobs available depends on the general state of the construction industry. With further training you can become a gas fitter or a central heating specialist; you can study for the Advanced Craft Certificate and (if you have some academic ability) you can train as a technician plumber which will stand you in good stead to move into a supervisory job — although it is quite possible that you may encounter some degree of reluctance to employ women in senior positions.

Flexibility When you've gained sufficient experience you may want to go into business on your own, which would enable you to become more independent and to regulate your working hours to some extent. It shouldn't be too difficult to return to work after a break of a few years.

Pay Poor while training, then medium to high.

Airline Pilot

The best general source of information is the Civil Aviation Authority, FCL3, Shell Mex House, Strand, London WC2.

You may also find the British Women's Pilots' Association helpful. Address: British Airways Terminus, P.O. Box 13, London SW1.

The work   The most taxing part of a pilot's job is to read, assimilate and process the mass of information which comes from the instrument panel in front of her, from radio messages through her headphones, and from her colleagues in the flight crew. Her ability to make decisions quickly and calmly is all-important. If there's an instrument failure she may suddenly have to take over from the automatic pilot or she may have to take swift evasive action to avoid a mid-air collision. She must be able to deal at any time with a potentially catastrophic emergency, although she gets little or no real practice, as it is unlikely ever to happen! She must be able to make endless, repetitive checks without getting lulled into carelessness by boredom or familiarity – and keep constantly alert during long flights.

To be a pilot you need self-confidence, leadership qualities, a quick, agile brain and an excellent memory. You must be able to fight boredom, take instant decisions and have a well-balanced personality. You will need to work irregular hours and, depending on which routes you are flying, you may have to spend long periods away from home. (It is worth pointing out, however, that two of Dan Air's women pilots have managed to carry on working while bringing up children.) You must have excellent physical health, lots of stamina and perfect eyesight.

Training   Schemes vary from one airline to another and the number of training places available varies from year to year, so the best way to start is by writing to all the British airlines to find out about their current arrangements. You will find their addresses in the *Flight Directory of British Aviation* which should be available in the reference section of a public library. These days it is so expensive to train (it cost £5000 when Marilyn Booth did it, but is now getting on for *four* times that amount!) that sponsorship from an airline is essential.

As a basic qualification you should have at least two A-levels (one of which is a science subject) and three O-levels. Graduates, particularly in science or engineering, stand the best chance of getting accepted, but as Marilyn demonstrated, it's not absolutely necessary to have a degree – you may just make the break by being in the right place at the right time. Men who learn to fly with the RAF have a big advantage over women: the greatest source of discrimination in this particular line of work is the refusal (so far) of the WRAF to train women as pilots.

The training lasts about 20 months; you may have to repay some of the cost (gradually) when you have qualified.

Prospects While it is difficult to get trained in the first place, the prospects are good once you've got over that hurdle – as long as you keep in good health and pass the regular efficiency tests. Your seniority depends upon the length of your flying experience and the number of different aircraft you can fly. If you don't want to fly with civil airlines (or if you can't get a job with one of them) you may be able to get work in aerial photography, crop spraying, weather and traffic observation; as an instructor or as a pilot of private planes employed by an individual, company or club.

Flexibility If you have a short break in your career, you will lose seniority, but as long as you pass the medical and efficiency tests, you should be able to get back to work.

Pay Medium to very high.

Related fields

Helicopter Pilots fly air taxi services, supply oil rigs, observe traffic, etc. Enquiries to the British Helicopter Advisory Board, Knowles House, Cromwell Road, Redhill, Surrey.

Air Traffic Control enquiries to the Civil Aviation Authority (address on p.120).

Sales Representative

Source of general information: The Institute of Marketing, Moor Hall, Cookham, Maidenhead, Berks SL6 9QH.

The work This obviously varies a great deal depending on what you are selling and to whom. Just about everything has to be sold – from food and clothing to engineering goods, books and insurance. Some representatives sell to wholesalers or to retail shops; this often involves helping the retailer to maximize sales by means of promotion campaigns, improved displays, new sales techniques, etc. Others do specialist selling not to shopkeepers or store buyers but to financial or technical experts. To do this you usually need specialist knowledge, if not formal training.

A sales rep may be part of a team or the only one in her firm. In big organizations, sales reps work under sales supervisors and area sales managers who in turn answer to sales managers and directors. A representative may have a large or small territory, depending on the product and the organization. Export sales reps travel extensively.

Some reps get commission for what they sell – *ie* a percentage of the value of the goods they have sold. Others get paid just a salary. To be a rep you need an extrovert personality, lots of confidence, an ability to establish instant rapport with strangers, indifference to rebuff, the capacity to enjoy being alone for long periods while on the road and a fair degree of numeracy.

Training   There is no standard way of becoming a sales representative and there are no basic qualifications. You may start working for a company as a clerk and move on to selling (as Liane Bracken did); or you may join a company as a trainee, graduate or non-graduate. Big companies run their own training schemes; small companies often give no formal training at all.

Prospects   Generally good, especially as more companies are cottoning on to the idea that women are good at selling all sorts of things, not just cosmetics! Experience as a sales rep forms a useful basis for a career in marketing (*ie* the overall management of selling goods) and that can lead to top jobs in management. Selling is a field where success depends a lot upon your own confidence and the ability to show initiative and seize opportunities as they arise; otherwise it could be a dreary dead-end.

Flexibility   The job may be flexible once you have proved your worth, but that will depend upon the individual company. The job is not generally geared to suit women with young children.

Pay   Medium to high.

Related fields

Marketing   Institute of Marketing (address on p.121).

Public Relations   Institute of Public Relations, 1 Great James Street, London WC1N 3DA.

Advertising   Institute of Practitioners in Advertising, 44 Belgrave Square, London SW1.

Retail Distribution   Distributive Industry Training Board, McLaren House, Talbot Road, Stretford, Manchester M32 0FP.

Astronomer

The British Astronomical Association, Burlington House, London W1, publishes a booklet *Astronomy as a Career*.

The Civil Service Commission, Alençon Link, Basingstoke, Hampshire, can provide information on jobs in astronomy and physics.

The work   Astronomy is a small, highly specialized branch of physics. What few jobs there are occur in universities and in the Civil Service. There are various branches of astronomy, as Jocelyn Burnell indicates (between pp.63–70). Some astronomers study the ionosphere and the earth's immediate environment; some study stars visible by telescope; others study stars in this galaxy and beyond, which are not visible but emit various signals such as radio waves and x-rays. The work is slow, intricate and pains-taking; exciting discoveries such as Jocelyn's are very rare. To become an astronomer you will need not only a passionate interest in the subject but good academic qualifications and an aptitude for research, as well as imagination.

Training   You need a good degree in physics or astronomy and further training, usually by way of a Ph.D.

Prospects and Flexibility   Impossible to generalize.

Pay   Medium to high.

Physics

While jobs in astronomy are relatively few, a university degree in physics is a very useful starting qualification for a wide range of jobs. The Institute of Physics, 47 Belgrave Square, London SW1X 8QX, provides a leaflet *Careers with Physics*, and other free publications. For a list of degree courses and the options they include, read *Degree Course Guide – Physics*, published by the Careers Research and Advisory Council (CRAC), Bateman Street, Cambridge (you may find it in your local Careers Office or public library).

There are good opportunities for physicists in industry, working in research and development, quality control, production, technical writing or sales and services. Alternatively, you may find interesting work with Government-sponsored bodies such as the UK Atomic Energy Authority, in forensic science laboratories, or in research jobs attached to universities. There are jobs for medical physicists in hospital laboratories; physicists also work in the fields of geophysics and meteorology.

Prospects   Generally good, especially if you put your physics to practical use, *eg* in engineering. In industry you may have an opportunity to move into management.

Pay   Medium to high.

Related fields

Engineering (see p.108), computer programming, metallurgy, materials science, environmental science, chemical physics, cybernetics, systems analysis. There is a good summary of areas of work for professional scientists in *The Scientist*, No.100 in the *Choice of Careers* series published by HMSO.

Car Mechanic

Information can be obtained from the Road Transport Industry Training Board, Capitol House, Empire Way, Wembley, Middlesex.

The Institute of the Motor Industry, Fanshaws, Brickenden, Herts, publishes a career booklet obtainable free of charge, *You and the Motor Industry*.

The work   Car mechanics do a lot more than wield a spanner. As the IMI booklet explains, apprentice mechanics learn about 'measuring instruments such as steering, tracking, suspension and engine test gauges, wheel balancers and brake meters; properties and behaviour under heat of metals used in vehicle construction when under repair, and the applications of welding; simple principles of the internal combustion engine, carburation and ignition; lighting, suspension, braking, transmission and steering'. They also learn how to 'use the instruments mentioned above; use all the tools required for maintenance or repair work; read simple blueprints including wiring diagrams; quickly diagnose faults and symptoms; know the best methods for rectifying faults; "test and tune"; fit to recognised limits components such as bearings, gears, pins and bushes, ball bearings, cylinder liners, pistons and clutches'.

As a car mechanic you need to be physically fit and reasonably strong (though not unusually so); to be interested in mechanical matters; to enjoy manual work and not mind getting dirty.

Training   You will need to have attained a reasonable educational standard in maths and science. O-level or good CSE passes in these subjects will be a help. The most common way of starting as a car mechanic is by finding a firm to take you on as an apprentice. The apprenticeship usually lasts four years, combining practical experience with part-time study, and leads to the National Craft Certificate. TOPS (p.92) provides a useful alternative entry, especially since some employers are still reluctant to take on girl apprentices.

Prospects   Good. Skilled mechanics are always in demand. After some experience you may progress to become a reception engineer providing the main link between the customer and the garage; or you may move on to selling vehicles or managing garages or retail outlets. With further study you can become a technician, commanding higher pay, with the possibility of promotion to supervisor. In this line of work, however, you may encounter a reluctance to employ women in senior positions. With enough experience and some capital, you might set up your own garage.

Flexibility   Once you have qualified, a break in your employment should not cause too many difficulties.

Pay   Poor to medium, occasionally high.

Other jobs in the motor industry

Mechanics may specialize in service and repair of lorries and trucks, motorcycles and racing cars, buses and coaches. There are also jobs in body repairing, panel beating, painting and spraying, and servicing of vehicles' electrical systems. Details of all these from the Road Transport Industry Training Board (address on p.124).

Vehicle Engineer   A specialist branch of mechanical engineering, divided into three tiers: professional, technician and craft (see pp.106–9). Vehicle engineers often work in factories rather than garages. Craft-level jobs include auto-electrician, coach builder, vehicle body builder, electroplater, sheet metal worker, spray painter, upholsterer and welder. Information from the Engineering Industry Training Board, 54 Clarendon Road, Watford WD1 1LB.

Accountant

Main sources of information:

Institute of Chartered Accountants in England and Wales, P.O. Box 433, Chartered Accountants' Hall, Moorgate Place, London EC2R 6EQ.

Institute of Chartered Accountants in Scotland, 27 Queen Street, Edinburgh EH2 1LH.

Institute of Chartered Accountants in Ireland, 7 Fitzwilliam Place, Dublin 2.

The Association of Certified Accountants, 22 Bedford Square, London WC1.

The work   Accountants work for many organizations, from commercial companies, banks and local authorities to voluntary organizations and trade unions, but wherever they work their function is essentially the same. They are concerned with the management of money: book-keeping, budgeting, taxation, preparation of accounts, auditing, and giving financial advice. They often meet a lot of people in the course of their work and some travel widely. They work either in private firms or partnerships; in industry or commerce; or in local government or other public bodies.

As an accountant you need to be good with figures (obviously!); to have a logical mind, good business sense, patience in dealing with detail and a liking for desk work.

Training   You need two A-levels and three O-levels including maths and English language. To train as a *chartered accountant* if you do not have a recognized degree, you must:

a) take a nine-month full-time Foundation course at a polytechnic; then

b) undertake a four-year 'training contract' (often called articles) with a firm of chartered accountants. During this time you will be given 22 weeks' leave to study for the qualifying exams.

If you are a graduate, your 'training contract' lasts three years and you will probably be exempt from the Foundation course. Whether graduate or not, you must stay with the same firm of chartered accountants throughout your training.

The training to become a *certified accountant* follows similar lines but is more flexible. Instead of a 'training contract' you study for the qualifying exams in your own time, while working for four years (or three for graduates) as a salaried employee either in an approved accountancy department in industry, in the public sector, or with a certified accountant in private practice. You can switch employers during the training and you are not obliged to take the Foundation course.

Qualification as a chartered accountant attracts more prestige, but the two methods of training qualify you to do the same work.

If you want to work chiefly in industry or commerce you may find it more useful to follow the training syllabus of the Institute of Cost and Management Accountants, 63 Portland Place, London W1N 4AB.

If you want to work chiefly in the public sector, you can follow the training syllabus of the Chartered Institute of Public Finance and Accountancy, 1 Buckingham Place, London SW1.

Prospects   Excellent. Even at a time of economic depression, accountants are much in demand. There are good opportunities to advance into highly paid senior positions and plenty of scope to move sideways into banking, management, management consultancy, systems analysis, etc.

Flexibility   Some part-time work is available. A break in your career should present few problems. You may be able to work from home (see p.83).

Pay   Once qualified, medium to high.

Related fields

Banking   Banking Information Service, 10 Lombard Street, London EC3V 9AR.

Computing   British Computer Society, 29 Portland Place, London W1N 3AG.

Insurance   The Careers Information Officer, The Chartered Insurance Institute, The Hall, 20 Aldermanbury, London EC2V 7HY.

Purchasing and Supply   Institute of Purchasing and Supply, York House, Westminster Bridge Road, London SE1.

Statistics   Institute of Statisticians, 36 Churchgate Street, Bury St Edmunds, Suffolk.

Tax inspection   Civil Service Commission, Alençon Link, Basingstoke, Hampshire.

Park Gardener

General information from the Agricultural Training Board (which also covers gardening), Bourne House, 32–34 Beckenham Road, Beckenham, Kent BR3 4PB.

Other useful sources: the Royal Horticultural Society, Vincent Square, London SW1.

Women's Farm and Garden Association, Courtland House, Byng Place, London WC1.

Agriculture and Horticulture, No. 85 in the HMSO *Choice of Careers* series.

Specific information about jobs and apprenticeships in parks from the personnel department of local authorities.

The work   'Amenity horticulture' is the fancy term applied to park gardening. The purpose is to provide and maintain pleasant open-air environments for relaxation and recreation. 'Amenities' include parks, picnic areas, National Trust properties, nature trails, bowling greens, playing fields.

The other 'branch' of gardening is crop production, which is what Susan White does. However, you're more likely to find this type of work in privately owned market gardens, nurseries and fruit farms than in public parks. Obviously, there's no point going in for gardening unless you enjoy outdoor manual work.

Training There are various training schemes run by local authorities, royal parks, the Greater London Council, the Royal Botanical Gardens, etc. Some CSE or O-level passes may be required. The standard method of training is by apprenticeship, combining practical experience with day-release or block-release study, leading to exams which give you a craft qualification. One-year courses leading to horticulture certificates are available under TOPS (p.92).

Prospects Fair. If you're ambitious there are some opportunities for advancement to managerial positions in the public sector.

Flexibility Plenty of seasonal part-time work, but this will be outside any career structure.

Pay Poor to medium.

Related fields

Agriculture Agricultural Training Board, address on p.127.

Conservation See p.118.

Landscape Architecture The Secretary, Landscape Institute, 12 Carlton House Terrace, London SW1Y 5AH.